PORTFOLIO
GORAS AND DESIS

An economist, Omkar Goswami secured his DPhil from Oxford in 1982. From then to 1996, he researched and taught at the Delhi School of Economics, Tufts, Jawaharlal Nehru University, Rutgers and the Indian Statistical Institute, and was a consultant to the World Bank, the Asian Development Bank and the Organisation for Economic Co-operation and Development. After a period as the editor of *Business India*, Omkar was chief economist at the Confederation of Indian Industry. Since 2004, he runs a corporate and economic consulting firm called CERG Advisory, and serves on the boards of some major listed companies. His passions are music, mountain walks, incessant reading, theatre and films.

GURCHARAN DAS is a world-renowned author, commentator and public intellectual. His bestselling books include *India Unbound*, *The Difficulty of Being Good* and *India Grows at Night*. His other literary works consist of a novel, *A Fine Family*, a book of essays, *The Elephant Paradigm*, and an anthology, *Three Plays*. A graduate of Harvard University, Das was CEO of Procter & Gamble, India, before he took early retirement to become a full-time writer. He lives in Delhi.

THE STORY OF INDIAN BUSINESS
Series Editor: Gurcharan Das

THE STORY OF INDIAN BUSINESS

GORAS AND DESIS

*Managing Agencies and the
Making of Corporate India*

OMKAR GOSWAMI

Introduction by
Gurcharan Das

PORTFOLIO
PENGUIN

An imprint of Penguin Random House

PORTFOLIO

USA | Canada | UK | Ireland | Australia
New Zealand | India | South Africa | China | Singapore

Portfolio is part of the Penguin Random House group of companies
whose addresses can be found at global.penguinrandomhouse.com

Published by Penguin Random House India Pvt. Ltd
4th Floor, Capital Tower 1, MG Road,
Gurugram 122 002, Haryana, India

Penguin
Random House
India

First published in Portfolio by Penguin Random House India 2016

ISBN 9780143425359

Typeset in Aldine401 BT by Manipal Digital Systems, Manipal

Printed at Manipal Technologies Limited, India

www.penguin.co.in

This is a legitimate digitally printed version of the book and therefore might not
have certain extra finishing on the cover.

*To Radhika, for her love and everlasting support,
and to young Samar, who gives such unalloyed joy*

CONTENTS

A TIMELINE

Years	Events
1813	The East India Company Act legislated in Britain. It renews the charter of the Company, but takes away almost all monopoly trading rights. Thus opens door for private merchants, traders and agency houses in India
1820–1840	Growth of British mercantile agency houses in Calcutta, and British and Parsi firms in Bombay, most of them trading in opium, cotton, textiles, saltpetre and other such goods
1834	Carr, Tagore & Company, the first real managing agency in India, formed by Dwarkanath Tagore in Calcutta
1854	First cotton mill set up in Tardeo, Bombay, by a Parsi, C.N. Davar

1855	First jute mill set up in Rishra, near Calcutta, by a Scot, George Ackland
1857, 1858	The Sepoy Mutiny (or the First Indian War of Independence). On 1 November 1858, governance of British India moves from East India Company to the Crown
1880–1914	All major British managing agencies in operation in Calcutta, controlling jute mills, collieries, tea gardens and coastal and inland waterways shipping. So too all major Indian managing agencies in Bombay and Ahmedabad controlling cotton mills
1907, 1912	Shares of Tata Iron and Steel successfully floated across India in August 1907. Mill rolls its first steel ingot in February 1912
1914–1918	World War I. Huge profits for the jute and cotton mills
1920	First Indian jute mill set up by G.D. Birla under Birla Brothers
1921–29	Post-war boom. Major growth for jute, cotton and tea. Tata Iron and Steel grows under a regime of 'discriminating protection'
1930–35	The Great Depression. Creates havoc for tea and jute industries. But has no effect on either cotton textiles or iron and steel
1936	Some constraints imposed upon managing agencies by the Companies Act, 1936

1939–45	World War II, and large profits again for jute mills
1947	India gains independence. Most jute-growing areas go to East Pakistan, the mills remain in India
1956	Companies Act, 1956, puts further checks on managing agencies
1956–1961	Second Five Year Plan, which sees the growth of many large state-owned enterprises: integrated steel plants, dams, fertilizer plants, heavy engineering and electrical projects. Significant growth in new investments by large Indian business houses
1960s	Exit of most British managing agencies in India and takeover by Indian business houses
1970	The managing agency system formally abolished on 3 April

INTRODUCTION

India has contributed an unusual entrepreneurial business organization to the world called the 'managing agency'. Its structure allowed the partners in the firm (usually few in number) to control with minimum capital a vast number of large independent joint stock operating companies. Its competitive advantage lay in the autonomy it gave to its decision makers and its access to risk capital. As a result of quick decision-making, it was able to tap new opportunities that opened up in nineteenth-century India at minimal personal risk to its partners. This structure was so successful that it went on to dominate the industrial capital of India for a century and a half. But in the end it suffered from conflicts of interest, and once capital became abundant and a managerial class developed, its utility became questionable. After some highly publicized governance scandals, the socialist government of Indira Gandhi abolished the managing agency system in 1970.

Ah . . . To Be Light-footed, Nimble and Free!

The managing agency system evolved in the second quarter of the nineteenth century as an answer to the scarcity of venture capital, lack of trained managers, undeveloped capital markets and political uncertainty. Here is how the system worked: the managing agency was the entrepreneur; when it saw an opportunity, say a jute mill, it quickly raised venture capital from friends and partners of the managing agent or promoter, borrowing the rest from a bank; with this money the agency set up the jute mill; once it tasted some success with the mill, it sold its majority shareholding in the venture to the public; the proceeds were now invested in, let's say, a tea garden. Meanwhile, the agency continued to manage the jute company, despite its small shareholding, as a result of a long-term management contract with the company. In this way, a managing agency was able to control a number of enterprises with only a small financial stake in each. It made the key managerial decisions on behalf of its operating companies about what products to make, what markets to seek and what raw materials to exploit.

A managing agency's ability to raise capital from a bank or from the public was in direct proportion to its track record and reputation. It also had access to the reserves of its managed companies, which it employed to fund new enterprises or subsidize dividends of its less successful ones. The managed companies, in turn, benefitted from (1) the low costs of a lean, common management, (2) economies of scale in the purchase of common raw materials and (3) access to common marketing networks in the sale of products. The partners of the agency had a high appetite for entrepreneurship because they earned generous commissions, either as a percentage of sales (in the early years) or profits (later on), plus other fees and cuts on purchases and sales. Best of all, the managing agency was light-footed, nimble and free for much of its existence.

With all these advantages, managing agencies were quickly successful, and the innovative structure became popular both with British *gora* and Indian *desi* business communities; it went on to guide India's entry into modern industry, trade and commercial agriculture over the next century and a half. By the First World War, managing agencies controlled 75 per cent of the industrial capital of India and accounted for half the industrial employment. As late as in 1954, managing agencies accounted for 51 per cent of the share capital of all companies.

Why Goswami's Book Is Unique

Beginning with the nationalist historians, most commentators condemned the managing agency system for its high commissions, its conflicts of interest and its furthering of Britain's colonial project. After Independence, the commentary shifted to the managing agencies' failure in corporate governance. There were inherent problems in their very structure, of course, given the separation of ownership and control. Since the shareholder's interest was subservient to the agent's, a few agents did abuse their position, acting in their own interest rather than the shareholder's. The vast majority of these agencies, however, acted in good faith, built trust and contributed vastly to the economic development of India.

Omkar Goswami's fine study of this industrial organization is refreshingly different. Rather than focus on the old debates, he is interested in the question: 'how good an entrepreneur was the managing agency?' His book examines this form of entrepreneurship in the context of the times, when the colonial government began to build roads and railways, abolished internal customs tariffs, established a legal system, enforced property rights and curbed the power of government to act in an arbitrary fashion.

These were some of the factors that propelled an unusual Bengali, Dwarkanath Tagore (grandfather of Rabindranath Tagore) to create with his English partner the first genuine managing agency in 1834. He played a pioneering role in establishing a new entrepreneurial organization that tapped the fresh opportunities that were opening up in coal mining, inland water transport, modern banking, etc. Goswami narrates Dwarkanath's rise and fall with great panache. 'It is ironical that a system whose invention is always attributed to British mercantile houses and associated with colonialism should have begun with an Indian-owned firm,' wrote Dwarkanath's biographer Blair Kling.

Why Did Indians Adopt This Managerial Organization?

The roots of this organizational structure lie in the decline of the East India Company. When the Company lost its trading monopoly, space opened up for others with enterprise. The first among them were the Company's former servants, who set up their own trading agencies. Legendary names such as Gillanders, Arbuthnot & Co. and Jardine Skinner go back to those days. Besides trading, these old agency houses slowly started other activities—for example, they began to advance money to indigo manufacturers, receiving the manufactured dye on consignment for sale in Europe. As Goswami explains, the great surge in managing agencies, however, came after the British took over India's governance from the East India Company after the 1860s. Thus were born the famous managing agencies Mackinnon, Mackenzie, Andrew Yule, Bird and Co., Shaw Wallace, Martin, Burn and many others who went on to dominate Calcutta's 'burra sahib' business landscape for a century.

This innovative organization also caught the imagination of Indian entrepreneurs, especially Parsis and Gujaratis, who set up the first cotton textile mills in western India to compete with Lancashire. The Tatas built the country's first steel plant at the turn of the century and the Birlas moved into jute manufacturing after World War I. There were many others too, who adopted the managing agency system avidly as the business organization of choice. Although British merchants in

India had pioneered it, Indians quickly discovered its risk-mitigating entrepreneurial value. The managing agency system served as a bridge to help carry Indian enterprise from traditional trading and moneylending to modern industry.

For centuries, business in India has been concentrated in the hands of trading communities, the vaishyas, who have run it as a family firm. Typically, the eldest male managed the organization with the help of other family members and the sympathetic support of his community. Business families arose from the bazaar through trade and moneylending, and over time they were responsible for a number of outstanding trading and financial innovations— the *hundi*, a bill of exchange that facilitated mobile credit and long-distance remittance; the *goladari*, a warehouse receipt financing; *fatka*, a sophisticated trading system in the futures market; *teji-mandi*, a contract for put and call options; and in recent times, rotating savings-and-credit funds such as chits, *nidhi*s and *kuri*es.

The managing agency structure played to their strength as innovative financiers. It provided them a low-risk means to either buy existing weak industrial enterprises or start new ones. Once the colonial government extended a degree of protection after the First World War, they invested exuberantly their wartime profits in emerging industrial opportunities. Suddenly, they became proud industrialists. In the process, however, they skipped the long and hard learning curve of technological innovation that had brought the industrial revolution to the West. They had not got their hands dirty on the shop floor;

nor had they spent long hours in the laboratory to come up with a new product. Their approach was a practical one. Why reinvent the wheel when you can buy the latest technology? As a result, the ethic of technological innovation has eluded Indian industry. The managing agency system is partly responsible for this—it made it too easy for a trader/financier to transform into an industrialist.

Over Time Gora Agencies Weakened and Desis Prospered

Before the First World War, the British managing agencies had been in a safe zone. Although they had diversified into coal mining, jute and tea plantations, their mainstay was the steady import of cotton piece-goods from the mills of Lancashire. The piece-goods trade was attractive to the British managing agency as it entailed low capital, brought swift returns, and much of the risk was borne by their junior Indian partners, the *banian*s. From the mills of Bombay and Ahmedabad, Indian textiles had begun to present tough competition, but the Indian market was also expanding rapidly, and there was room for everyone. After the War, however, things changed dramatically. The colonial government introduced tariff protection, in line with rising protectionism around the world, and it opened up opportunities for domestic manufacturing.

Indian entrepreneurs, through their managing agencies, jumped into the fray, as Goswami has explained. In Bombay and Ahmedabad, the Indians already had a strong grip over the cotton textile industry. After the First World War, they began manufacturing jute, sugar, iron and steel, cement, chemicals, engineering and food processing products. But the Calcutta-based gora managing agencies failed to seize the opportunity. They remained in their comfort zone. Ironically, many of them had been dynamic and full of entrepreneurial energy for half a century, from 1840 to 1890. But over time, they lost their energy and became rigid members of a self-satisfied Calcutta burra sahib colonial society. When opportunity came after the First World War, they remained stuck in a cocoon. The partnership form also limited their capital and their ambitions. They might have overcome these constraints by forming joint ventures with Indians, but their historical sense of racial and social exclusivity came in the way, as Maria Misra has pointed out so perceptively. Meanwhile, desi managing agencies expanded and prospered in the inter-war years, as did many multinational companies who came into India.

The managing agency system also failed to evolve. It had always held out great potential; it ought to have integrated its managed companies closer, somewhat like subsidiaries of a modern diversified multinational group and enjoyed thereby the benefits of synergy. This might have helped it move up a notch in competitiveness and take on multinational companies that had begun to spring up around the world. But it failed to do so. The parent managing agencies never seemed to give their children, the managed companies, the autonomy that would have helped them become single-mindedly more focused and better able to compete in the market. The best-managed, diversified conglomerates of today are aware of the power of focus, the reason why they give significant operational freedom to their subsidiaries.

Managing agencies also failed to separate ownership from control. As a result, they did not develop sufficient professional managers in their managed companies, which became uncompetitive over time. Even within their own managing agencies, they did not realize the power of functional expertise—they did not recruit enough technical specialists who could have solved technical problems across their managed companies. The Indian managing agencies did overcome some of these flaws, but in the end both the desi agencies and the British burra sahib agencies remained creatures of their own history. They failed to evolve with the times and did not fully capitalize on the opportunities that opened up in the twentieth century.

Mounting Corporate Governance Problems

Shareholders of both desi and gora enterprises began to grow restive after the 1920s, especially during the Depression and up to the Second World War. As markets became more competitive, their profitability declined, and so did the dividends to shareholders. Reports also appeared of unscrupulous managing agencies abusing their power to enrich themselves at the expense of shareholders in their managed companies. Some of the Ahmedabad and Bombay managing agencies attempted to reform managing agency contracts by moving from commissions on sales or production to commissions on profits, which helped to align the incentive system of the managing agency closer to that of the managed company. The British agencies dragged their feet and followed suit, if they did, only after the Depression. Shareholders remained discontented but powerless because their individual shareholding was too small. A few did raise the obvious question: why weren't managing agents being replaced with professional managers who would be supervised by an independent board?

The problem of control versus ownership is not unique to managing agencies. It is a universal 'agency problem' between managers and owners in any capitalist enterprise where shareholding is diffused. Even the pioneering East India Company faced it, as we saw in Tirthankar Roy's volume in our *The Story of Indian Business* series. Much contemporary reform of corporate boards around the world has been driven by the need for better oversight to make managements more accountable to shareholders. In the case of managing agencies, the problem was compounded by conflicts of interest inherent in their basic structure, which allowed managing agents to transfer shares between independent companies and permitted them to start new enterprises with capital raised from the public for a different purpose.

As a result of shareholder clamour, amendments were made to the Company Law, curbing the independence of managing agencies in 1936. As a result, shareholders could 1) remove managing agents who had been guilty of offences; 2) limit their compensation; and 3) curb their ability to transfer funds from one company to another. The chorus of condemnation became louder after Independence. In 1964, R.K. Hazari, who later headed a powerful government committee for regulating business, said in a well-known document commonly referred to as the Hazari Report: 'This form of management is not necessary for providing firm and stable group control over management. It does not, in general, bring about economies of management. On the contrary, it is an expensive and irrational system of management to which the managing agents do not even devote their whole time. The abolition of the system is necessary in order to rationalize the management of public industrial companies.'

How This System Fostered India's Development

It is not easy to be a pioneer. The first entrepreneurs who tried to set up cotton textile mills in Bombay and Ahmedabad failed to raise capital. Framji Cowasji Banaji was one of them—he found it impossible to find financial backers in Bombay in 1845. So did Ranchhodlal Chotalal in Ahmedabad. For good reason: out of the hundred or so textile mills that came up in Bombay between 1854 and 1925, forty-five went bankrupt and had to be sold. The managing agency system came about partially as a response to the high risks in starting a new enterprise in an emerging market. It helped to spread the risk of failure for an investor.

As noted, the managing agent was the entrepreneur. His initial task was to raise capital. He usually put down some of his own money, borrowing the rest from friends or from the public via equity or interest-bearing deposits. Over time, his ability to raise capital depended on his track record and his reputation. With the initial capital, he acquired land and machinery, and supervised construction of the factory. Next, he hired workers and purchased cotton and other raw materials. Once manufacturing started, the agent sought markets for sale of the mill's product.

The managing agency system rewarded the agent for this pioneering work by assuring him a regular monthly income, topped up with a commission on sales and purchases even before the business had made any profit. Once profits came, he gained as one of the largest shareholders of the business. Thus, setting up a new enterprise became a more and more attractive proposition, encouraging managing agents to become serial entrepreneurs. The cotton textile business thus proliferated rapidly in Bombay and Ahmedabad in the second half of the nineteenth century. Over time, for some managing agencies, the commissions also became risk-based, as we have noted, hinging on profits rather than on sales or production.

Some have argued that the managing agency system hindered India's development. I disagree. At an early stage, it played a vital role in India's industrialization. It is not surprising that both English and Indian businesses avidly adopted it and the system remained popular for more than a century. Some agents might have been obsessed with their commissions but most business people were driven by reputation in the marketplace. Lalbhai Kasturbhai, one of the most respected and successful Indian industrialists, expressed it well: 'The desire for maintaining one's reputation is so keen that no sooner there is a depression or the mill has not made profits, [than] the [managing agents] leave off [read 'relinquish'] half or full commission.'

Lalbhai was right. Business is ultimately based on reputation, as it leads to trust in the marketplace. This is a fundamental lesson that has been reinforced in volume after volume in *The Story of Indian Business*. The managing agency system would not have endured were it not for the trust reposed by investors in the managing agents.

The Story of Indian Business

We are accustomed to thinking of business in terms of people who get rich. We rarely think of the underlying institutions that produce wealth. This book on the managing agency system is an example of one such institution that came into existence after the decline of the East India Company and died quietly after India's independence, having outlived its usefulness. It is only one example of many that have engaged the authors of our unique multi-volume history of Indian business. This series as a whole is attempting to mine great ideas in business and economics that have shaped commerce in the bazaars and on the high seas of the Indian Ocean.

In these stories, leading contemporary scholars and writers examine historical texts, inscriptions and records, and interpret them in a lively, sharp and authoritative manner for the intelligent reader who may have no prior background in the field. Each slender volume offers an enduring perspective on business enterprise in the past. It seeks to entertain and edify, avoiding the pitfall of simplistically cataloguing a set of lessons for our times. The value of the exercise is to promote a longer-term sensibility in the reader for her better understanding of the material bases of our present human condition and to think sensibly about our economic future. Taken together, the series celebrates the ideal captured in the ancient Indian goal of life called *artha*.

The series began with Tom Trautmann's reinterpretation for our times of the renowned treatise on the science of wealth, *Arthashastra*, which was authored almost 2,000 years ago and is considered the world's first manual on political economy. Kanakalatha Mukund took us south in the next volume, *The World of the Tamil Merchant*, to a beguiling time when one of the ports of south India was receiving one ship a day from Rome. Mukund has reconstructed this world, drawing on the epics *Silappadikaram*, *Manimekalai* and other historical materials, up to the end of the Chola empire. Next, we jumped some centuries to Tirthankar Roy's radiant account of the East India Company, which taught us, among other things, how much the modern multinational corporation is a child of the company that ruled India and is mostly reviled today.

Our fourth volume hopped to the late eighteenth century to the time of decline of the port of Surat and the rise of Bombay. In it, Lakshmi Subramanian recounted vividly the ups and downs in the adventurous lives of three merchants in *Three Merchants of Bombay*—Trawadi Arjunji Nathji, Jamsetjee Jeejeebhoy and Premchand Roychand. Arshia Sattar returned to India's classical past to narrate in the fifth volume the brilliant adventures of *The Mouse Merchant* and tales based on *Kathasaritsagara*, *Panchatanra* and other sources. In the next volume, Tom Timberg's *Marwaris* examined the bold, risk-taking world of India's most famous business community. It quickly became a popular bestseller. In the seventh volume, Scott Levi took us back to the early modern period and recounted the saga of Punjabi Khatri traders from Multan, who took caravans on the 'Silk Road' across the Himalayas to Central Asia and beyond to Russia from 1500 to 1850. After that, Chayya Goswami and Jaitirath Rao dived deep into the Indian Ocean of the eighteenth century to recount the tale of Gujarati merchants from Kachchh in the trade triangle of Mandvi–Muscat–Zanzibar.

In the future lies a veritable feast. Bibek Debroy will narrate the exciting story of the building of railways in nineteenth and twentieth century India. Professor Donald Davis will raise contemporary issues in the area of commercial and business law based on medieval commentaries by authors such as Vacaspati Mishra and Chandeshvara on the *Dharmasastras*. We have plans for volumes on tales of trade in Mughal India and another one on the Indian Ocean. Two other business communities, the Chettiars and the Parsis, will be featured in future volumes. Finally, Medha Kudaisiya will round out the series, recording a story of betrayal in the historic 'Bombay Plan' drawn by eminent industrialists in 1944–45 on the future shape of independent India's economy.

Gurcharan Das

PROLOGUE

In the first half of the eighteenth century, there was nothing to choose between the English East India Company with its trading outposts in Surat, Madras and Calcutta, the French in Pondicherry, Mahé and Chandernagore, and the Portuguese *Estado da India* at Goa, Daman and Diu. If anything, the Portuguese were more securely established than any other foreign power. The English Company's humdrum beginnings offered no hint of its lengthy and powerful rule across India in the years to come.

That changed in the south, with the English Company's forces under Robert Clive defeating the French under Joseph François Dupleix in a series of battles that strengthened British hold over Madras and its neighbourhood. It transformed much more significantly in the east, when the headstrong twenty-three-year-old Siraj ud-Daulah (1733–1757) succeeded his wise grandfather Alivardi Khan (1671–1756) as the Nawab of Bengal. Annoyed by the increasing military presence of the British, Siraj attacked and ran over the English

Company's bastion at Fort William in Calcutta in June 1756. Then happened the 'Black Hole' of Calcutta—the locking up of many of the surrendered British officers and ensigns in a small room for the night of 20 June, many of whom died of heat and suffocation. Soon enough, the Company retaliated.

In 1757, an army and fleet from Madras under the joint command of Admiral Charles Watson and the thirty-three-year-old Clive recaptured Calcutta, seized the French fort at Chandernagore, and then sailed up the Hooghly to a place just south of Murshidabad called Palashi (Plassey). Here, thanks to the superior weaponry of the British and the downright treachery of Siraj's commanders and trusted men such as Mir Jafar, Yar Lutuf Khan, Rai Durlabh, Omichund and the moncylending family of the Jagat Seths, Siraj's army was thoroughly defeated on 23 June 1757 in an encounter that lasted barely forty minutes. The battle of Plassey changed British history in India.

Captured in flight, Siraj was assassinated on 2 July 1757. Mir Jaffar, appointed as the next Nawab, was deposed soon enough in favour of Mir Qasim, who was then defeated in the Battle of Buxar in 1764. Now fully in charge of both Bengal and Bihar, the Company forced a treaty upon the Mughal Emperor Shah Alam in 1765 by which it was given the governance and revenue collecting rights, or the *diwani*, of Bengal, Bihar and Orissa.

With that started major British annexations and conquests throughout India. These did not arise out of carefully planned strategies but through the force of 'created' circumstances, as and when these occurred, backed up by superior military might. In the north, Benares was annexed in 1773; Ghazipur in 1775; the Rohilla Afghans were defeated in 1794; the Nawab of Oudh ceded Gorakhpur, Rohilkhand, Allahabad, Fatehpur, Kanpur, Mirzapur, Etah, Mainpuri and parts of Kumaon by 1801; what remained of Kumaon and Garhwal was captured after the Anglo-Nepal War of 1814; and the rest of the Doab, Delhi, Agra, and parts of Bundelkhand were occupied following British victory in the second Anglo-Maratha War (1803–05). After a somewhat long gap, the imperial juggernaut resumed with the Company's victory in the First Anglo-Sikh War (1845–46). This led to its securing the Jullundur Doab and Hazara in the Punjab, as well as Kashmir, which was later sold to Maharaja Gulab Singh of Jammu. Triumph in the Second Anglo-Sikh War (1848–49) was followed by the full-fledged annexation of the Punjab and the North-West Frontier Provinces. Berar came under the British in 1854. So too did Satara in 1848, and Nagpur and Jhansi in 1854 via 'the doctrine of lapse', under which the administration of any princely state whose ruler was deemed by the Company to be 'manifestly incompetent' or who died without a male heir could be taken over. Finally, Oudh, the last big territory in the north, was annexed in 1856, and its ruler Wajid Ali Shah exiled to Calcutta.

In the east, Assam was formally taken over in 1838. And in 1853, following the victory in the Anglo-Burmese War, lower Burma, including Rangoon, came under the Company's control.

In the west, Jaipur became a British protectorate as early as 1794; the rest of the princely states of Rajputana accepted British suzerainty in 1817, as did Cutch in 1818 and Baroda in 1819. Much of what was the Maratha kingdom and Gujarat were taken over after the Company's forces won the Third Anglo-Maratha War in 1818. Sind (now Sindh) was annexed in 1843, with General Charles Napier allegedly sending a telegram to his superiors with a pun in Latin, *'Peccavi'* which meant 'I have sinned'.

In the south, the Northern Circars, or the coastal region of what is now Andhra Pradesh, were annexed in 1760. The Nizam of Hyderabad accepted British suzerainty by signing a subsidiary alliance in 1798. Mysore fell in 1799 after the defeat of Tipu Sultan in the Battle of Seringapatnam. Arcot and Nellore were annexed in 1801, and Coorg in 1834. Thus, barring the Nizam's territory and the princely state of Travancore, the entire subcontinent fell under British rule.

By 1856, therefore, the political, military and administrative writ of the English East India Company ran throughout most of undivided India. The demise of its authority occurred a year after quelling of the Sepoy Mutiny in 1857—the first serious military challenge to British rule across many parts of northern India. On 2 August 1858, under the Government of India Act of 1858, the administration of the country transferred from the East India Company to the Crown.

For an enterprise so immersed in unceasing territorial conquests, the Company was remarkably focused on administration, especially as it was required to collect much-needed land revenues. In 1793, in his attempt to create 'a rule of property' and generate stable land revenues, Lord Cornwallis enacted the Permanent Settlement, which covered Bengal, Bihar and Orissa. Based on fixed rates of revenue for different types of land, and relying on the reasonableness of these rates, the expectation was that the system would create a wide-ranging class of progressive zamindars (landlords) who would have strong incentives to increase agricultural productivity and surplus. That did not happen in many instances. Many early zamindars failed to pay their dues, and their zamindari rights were then auctioned off to others. This, however, created a market for land revenue rights and, over time, successful zamindars such as Dwarkanath Tagore, a character in this book, became enormously wealthy people.

Realizing that much of southern and western India was cultivated by peasant-owners who historically enjoyed a one-to-one association with the revenue-collecting machinery, the Company was adroit enough to introduce a very different land revenue settlement in the Madras and Bombay Presidencies. Called the *ryotwari* system (from the word *raiyat*, the cultivator), it was a direct revenue-collecting relationship between the owner-cultivators and the government. More difficult to settle—for it involved recording the ownership rights of all peasants in a district, their lands and the crops they cultivated—the ryotwari system of land revenue administration was also more efficient for both the taxing and taxed than the zamindari system.

Besides land revenues, the Company focused on opium, which was produced in Malwa, eastern United Provinces and parts of Bihar, and indigo, which was cultivated in Bihar. In the absence of chemical dyes, indigo was the staple ingredient in Manchester and other parts of England for dyeing cloth dark blue. Opium was lucrative business, for it not only fed a rapidly growing addiction throughout China but also financed an equally fast-growing tea trade between China and Britain. In 1773, therefore, an opium monopoly was created, where all opium in east India, and later from Malwa, would be produced by the Company's factories and sold or auctioned by it to traders—initially in Calcutta and later in Bombay.

Then came two pieces of legislation from London, both in response to the dire financial strains that the Company had wrought upon itself through incessant military and administrative expansion. The first was the Charter Act of 1813 which, while granting the Company an extra lease of life for twenty years, deprived it of all trading monopolies barring tea and the China trade. This was followed two decades later by the Government of India Act of 1833, which also granted the Company another twenty years of political and administrative authority, but took away all its commercial functions, including the remaining trading monopolies.

That set the stage for the growth of British private commercial enterprise in India. Partnership firms came into being to serve as agency houses for import of cloth and export of opium, indigo and saltpetre. Most of these mercantile houses were small and could not survive the vicissitudes of the markets. Others made their fortune in the opium trade with China, and often served as intermediaries to repatriate the accumulated wealth of those Company servants who had made their fortunes in India. Still other agency houses were diversified enough to profitably trade on several accounts, enjoying commissions on each, their partners becoming expatriate India hands. Some of the firms belonging to the last lot transformed into managing agencies by the third quarter of the nineteenth century—which is the tale of this book.

1

SETTING THE STAGE

This is a short economic history of the development of corporate India from the last quarter of the nineteenth century until the present time through the lens of managing agencies. While seemingly unique to India, managing agencies proliferated under many different names and structures in many parts of Asia and Latin America. In its many incarnations, this entity allowed entrepreneurially driven partnerships, business houses and families to retain significant managerial and cash flow control over many publicly listed and unlisted companies despite their relatively low share ownership in these companies. To understand the genesis and popularity of the managing agency, it is worth reflecting upon two great inventions that created the basic structure of today's corporate world. The first was the concept of 'joint stock'; and the second, that of 'limited liability'.

Before the advent of joint stock, most firms were organized either as single-owner proprietorships or small partnerships, usually with two to four partners. Constrained by the limited capital they could raise, these businesses were typically small in size and limited in their ability to take risks. In an era where a few wrong business calls could result in huge personal losses and even long stints in filthy debtors' prisons, it was natural for proprietors and partners to be better safe than sorry.

Joint stock created divisibility. In doing so, it not only increased the number of shareholders but also allowed for a significant increase in paid-up capital. The risk capital of a joint stock enterprise comprised a large number of equity shares, each affordable enough to be attractive to many shareholders. Each shareholder owned such part of the company that was exactly in proportion to his or her shares, which were transferable and saleable to others without affecting the existence of the corporate entity. An early joint stock entity was the English East India Company, which was granted a royal charter by Elizabeth I on 31 December 1600. However, the first joint stock entity with freely tradable shares was the *Vereenigde Oostindische Compagnie* or the Dutch East India Company. Incorporated in 1602, it is rightly considered the world's first multinational corporation, and its shares were actively traded on the Amsterdam Stock Exchange.

Joint stock was necessary but not sufficient to create a commercial world led by corporations. There had to be a clear, legally recognized way of distinguishing between the assets and liabilities of a company and those of its shareholders. Thus emerged the concept of 'limited liability', which limited the liabilities of the owners of a company to what they owned in it—that is to say, up to the value of their shares. Although English common law of the fifteenth and sixteenth centuries conferred limited liability on selected monasteries and trade guilds in relation to their common properties, the first modern limited liability law was enacted by the state of New York in 1811, followed four decades later by England with the Limited Liability Act of 1855.

Armed with joint stock and limited liability, companies now became distinct legal entities owned by, yet sufficiently separated from, its shareholders. The body corporate could raise loans in its own name, backed by the company's assets and income flows; its debt liabilities fell on the company and not the owners; and its equity liabilities were limited to the value of the shares.

With these two inventions, the modern corporation was born.

Agency Costs

Great inventions often create their own hazards. So too did the concepts of joint stock and limited liability. A particularly pervasive risk is called 'agency costs', and needs a brief explanation, for it makes plain much of the concept and practice of managing agencies. In essence, agency cost relates to the cost that a 'principal'—whether a corporation, a person, group of persons or shareholders— has to bear when it hires an 'agent' or manager to act on its behalf. Because the two parties usually have different interests—with the agent generally possessing more information on the company—the principal cannot automatically ensure that the agent is always acting in the principal's best interests.

To appreciate this, let us for a moment delve into a world without taxes, and consider a proprietary firm called ABC & Company, owned by a man called Amar. In this firm, all costs are Amar's; all risks are his; and all gains are his. There is no incentive at all for Amar to inflate costs and reduce profits, or to siphon some of the firm's money into his own coffers. However, Amar knows that ABC & Company, being a proprietary firm, cannot expand any faster than its growth in profits. He wants to do better and increase the business. So he reaches out to two admiring friends—Akbar and Anthony—and sells to each of them 15 per cent of the shares of ABC & Company. Now Amar owns 70 per cent of ABC, Akbar 15 per cent and Anthony 15 per cent. Given his detailed knowledge of the business, Amar continues to run ABC (as the agent), with Akbar and Anthony being large but dormant shareholders (the principals).

Almost immediately, agency costs come into play. Since Akbar and Anthony know little or nothing of the business and are passive shareholders betting on Amar's proven entrepreneurial skills, there is now a temptation for Amar to cream off some funds from the 'middle'. The reason is simple enough. Suppose ABC's distributable profit was Rs 100. Amar's share would be Rs 70, and Akbar's and Anthony's Rs 15 each. If Amar could cleverly siphon Rs 10 of the profits into a small partnership firm owned by his wife and daughter that ostensibly provided some services to ABC, the profit would reduce to Rs 90. This is now to be shared according to the 70:15:15 rule, namely Rs 63 for Amar and Rs 13.50 each for Akbar and Anthony. But Amar, as the agent, has already siphoned off Rs 10. So he has actually received Rs 73, while Akbar and Anthony were shortchanged by Rs 1.50 each. If the two were sufficiently diligent, they could force Amar to reverse the accounts. But, as distanced shareholders, they will most likely not do so, remaining happy with their Rs 13.50, not knowing that Amar actually made the extra buck at the expense of their ignorance.

Of course, Amar need not resort to such subterfuge. Claiming that he is the only shareholder who knows every bit of the business, without whom ABC & Company could scarcely operate, Amar could draw up a ten-year contract that gives him a fixed, annual fee for operating the business, a small commission on sales and a larger one on profits. If Akbar and Anthony believe in Amar's entrepreneurial and risk-taking skills, and feel that Amar's upfront fees aren't excessive, they might agree to such a contract. Amar then sets up a new limited liability company called Amarsons Limited with himself, his wife and daughter as shareholders, which becomes the *agency* that will *manage* ABC & Company. If Amarsons also possesses Amar's shares, it will then earn from ABC & Company the fixed fee, the commission on sales and profits and, in good times, dividends on account of Amar's shares.

Amarsons Limited is a classic managing agency. It has leveraged Amar's entrepreneurial skills and industrial

knowledge to attract new shareholders to a firm called ABC
& Company that it controls. ABC & Company, on its part,
has given Amarsons the authority (*agency*) to run (*manage*)
ABC on their behalf. For doing this, the managing agency,
Amarsons Limited, receives a fixed fee, commissions on
sales, and profits and dividends. And if ABC does well in
the future, it can dilute Amar's ownership even further
to attract many more shareholders and create a situation
where Amarsons, as the promoter-managing agency, can
continue controlling the show even while owning as little
as 15–20 per cent of ABC's equity.

Such agency costs are common.[1] Most small
shareholders who invest their savings in corporate equity
based on the reputation of the promoter-cum-managing
agent and past corporate performance usually know little
of how a company is actually run—something that was
certainly true in the pre-Internet world, and isn't without
substance even today. They expect little else except a
stream of reasonable dividends and steady share price
appreciation. This creates fertile ground for many a crafty
income-earning arrangement between the widely held
listed corporation and one or more of the privately held
companies owned by the promoters. In the late nineteenth
century, and through much of the twentieth, so long as
such actions did not dramatically reduce dividends for the
ordinary shareholders, these were par for the course. This

[1] For what is still the best work on agency costs, see Michael
C. Jensen and William H. Meckling, 'Theory of the Firm:
Managerial Behavior, Agency Costs and Ownership Structure',
Journal of Financial Economics, 3(4), October 1976, pp. 305–360.

was especially so in countries where, for sociological and cultural reasons, corporate growth critically depended on the risk-taking abilities of a small, concentrated group of entrepreneurial castes or communities—which was quite often the case in the early and middle stages of economic development. It is not surprising, therefore, that the 'visible hand' of entrepreneurial groups with strong managerial and cash flow control over widely held or publicly listed companies was amply evident in the US up to the Great Depression; in the UK till the end of World War II; in France, Italy and Spain till much later; in Japan and South Korea till the 1980s; and in much of emerging Asia right up to recent times.

The Managing Agency

There can be no doubt about the groaning poverty and wretchedness of India in 1900, which continued right upto Independence in 1947 and beyond. Yet, despite the sepia-tinted images of famines, beggars and skeletal cows, the fact of the matter was that by the early years of the twentieth century, British India had in place all the institutions needed for relatively rapid commercial growth. There were major railway lines linking ports to the interior as well as to the main cities and towns of the country.[2] Steamship companies moved cargo and people along the Malabar and Coromandel coasts, Burma and

[2] For instance, almost all the major railway lines in India today existed during 1900–47.

the riverine tracts of Bengal. A reasonable, though not necessarily bountiful, supply of loanable funds as working capital and through bill discounting was available from several banks including the three Presidency banks— Bank of Bengal, Bank of Bombay and Bank of Madras— which eventually got merged into the Imperial Bank, precursor to the State Bank of India. Calcutta, Bombay and Ahmedabad had enough wealthy urban Indians whose savings were ripe for the wooing, and which were chased by pedigreed entrepreneurs for risk capital. There were two stock exchanges—the Bombay Stock Exchange that was established in 1875, the second in Asia after Tokyo, and the Ahmedabad bourse that came up in 1894. The Calcutta Stock Exchange followed in 1908. Besides, the mid-Victorian British raj possessed a satisfactory contractual and legal system and reasonably efficient and largely fair courts for adjudicating on commercial matters, especially in the Presidency towns.

With the US Civil War, India became a source of cotton for the mills in Lancashire, and was itself soon home to spinning mills, and subsequently composite textile mills, set up by Parsi and Gujarati entrepreneurs of Bombay and later, of Ahmedabad. Similarly, after the Crimean War forced the flax mills in Dundee to switch to jute grown in east Bengal, it didn't take long for canny Scottish businessmen to realise that gunny bag and cloth could be more profitably manufactured along the banks of the Hooghly around Calcutta, which led to the growth of India's jute manufacturing industry. There were railway lines to be built and operated across the country; sugar to be manufactured from cane that was being grown in the Punjab, the United Provinces and the Bombay Presidency; and tea to be cultivated, processed and exported from plantations in Assam, Darjeeling and the Dooars. None of these activities required great manufacturing skills and technology. There were steady profits to be made. What was needed was an organizational form to attract risk capital and arrange the manufacturing resources.

That form was the managing agency. Present from the latter half of the nineteenth century, a typical managing agency in India was a partnership or a closely held private limited company that leveraged its connections and entrepreneurial reputation to float different businesses across India—jute, coal, cotton, railway, banking, insurance, sugar, engineering and other companies. In the words of an economist of the mid-1930s, those 'who had any money to invest in industries were willing to put [it] . . . in any enterprise promoted or backed by a reputable firm of managing agents. The imprimatur of a managing agent was found essential for the flotation of any public limited company in India'.[3] The manner in which these privately held firms soon came to control most, if not all, large enterprises in colonial, and thereafter independent, India despite their limited share ownership is a story of corporate finesse. It was a story no less evident in pre- and post-World War II Japan, South Korea, Hong Kong and parts of Asia and Latin America.

[3] P.S. Lokanathan, *Industrial Organisation in India*, London, Allen & Unwin, 1935, henceforth Lokanathan (1935), p. 23.

As the promoter, a managing agency would announce the flotation of a publicly held company in any one of the major industries. Its entrepreneurial reputation would typically result in oversubscription of the ordinary shares and ensure that no single person or body corporate had a holding large enough to even remotely challenge the managing agency's control over the affairs of the company. Thereafter, the agency would acquire enough proxy votes of the small shareholders to speak for the majority of those present and voting in the company's first general meeting.[4] At that meeting, shareholders would ratify the company's board of directors consisting of partners of the managing agency and other trusted people; and the company would secure approval to formally appoint the managing agency to look after its affairs. For this service, the managing agency would charge healthy commissions on sales and profits, plus fees from several other services such as sales and purchases through related companies, brokerage on inland transportation and shipping, commissions on insurance policies bought from a firm controlled by the agency, and annual charges for the supply of senior managers. It was a brilliant method which

---

[4] Most general meetings of the managed companies were over in a few minutes—such was the control of these managing agencies. This was an observation of H.C. Waters, a partner in Orr Dignam & Company, the most important firm of solicitors in Calcutta which served all the British managing agencies. See Stephanie Jones, *Merchants of the Raj: British Managing Agency Houses in Calcutta Yesterday and Today*, MacMillan Press, 1992, henceforth Jones (1992), p. 2.

leveraged entrepreneurial reputation to ensure significant control of the managing agencies that well exceeded their cash flow rights over the listed companies, in which they had relatively small ownership.

By the early 1930s, large managing agents controlled several widely held, listed companies, with their share ownership between 6 per cent and 20 per cent in the relatively more capital-intensive jute and cotton mills, and rarely ever exceeding 50 per cent in the case of tea gardens and collieries, which needed far less investments.[5] Besides, the managing agencies reaped benefits from the complementarities across industries. For instance, in 1911, Andrew Yule & Company, one of the largest managing agencies in Calcutta, controlled six jute mills, eleven collieries, ten plantations, a steamship company and several other, smaller firms. Similarly, the other large group in east India, Bird (along with F.W. Heilgers, which it acquired in 1917), controlled ten jute mills, eighteen collieries, an engineering works company, a fire-clay unit and other sundry companies.[6]

Jute mills and steamers created demand for the collieries; steamer companies earned revenues by shipping raw jute from riverine east Bengal to the mills on the Hooghly. All goods in transit and assets were underwritten by the agency's insurance companies. The two largest inland steamer companies operating in Bengal

[5] Lokanathan (1935), p. 187.
[6] Amiya K. Bagchi, *Private Investment in India, 1900–1939*, Cambridge, Cambridge University Press, 1972, henceforth Bagchi (1972), p. 177.

were managed by Andrew Yule and Macneill—both
having substantial interests in jute manufacturing. They
saw to it that raw jute coming into the mills from east
Bengal was shipped in tugboats attached to their steamers,
and insured by their affiliated underwriting company,
often at a premium that was 10 per cent higher than the
going rates.[7]

However, it would be entirely wrong to associate
managing agencies, even of the pre-Independence era,
exclusively with the British. Throughout Bombay and
Ahmedabad, and later, Delhi and Madras, most of colonial
India's corporate enterprises were controlled by various
native Indian houses. There were Indians such as the Tatas,
Birlas, Wadias, Chunilal Mehta, Shri Ram, Thackersay
and Mooljee, Khatau and Makhanji, Piramal, and a couple
of Bengali managing agents who controlled the cotton
textile industry. Even in Calcutta, a city where corporate
life was more British-controlled than in any other part of
the country, the inter-war years saw rapid growth of Indian
managing agencies in jute and collieries. Only tea remained
stubbornly British throughout the raj and even after.

The Agency House and the Managing Agency

At this point, it is important to emphasize the
distinction between agency houses and managing agencies.

---

[7] Government of Bengal, *Report of the Bengal Jute Enquiry Committee
(Fawcus)*, Alipore, 1940, Vol. II, evidence of the Bengal Jute
Dealers Association, pp. 170–1 and p. 173.

Agency houses had existed for a long time, dating back to the 1780s when enterprising British employees of the East India Company, who made their money in 'shaking the pagoda tree', quit their services to enlarge and repatriate their fortunes by setting up agency houses that engaged in the growing global trade in indigo, opium, saltpetre, coal and, later, mill-made calico from Lancashire.[8] As trade grew, so too did the number of agency houses: from fifteen in 1790 to twenty-seven in 1828, and then to ninety-three in 1846.[9] They were exactly what their name suggested— partnerships that ran on agency commissions on export or import trade. Barring half a dozen or so that also conducted trading business on their own account, most were relatively tiny partnerships with short business lives.

Some larger mercantile agency houses eventually transformed into managing agencies in the second half of the nineteenth century. Two notable examples were Jardine Skinner & Company,[10] which had sizeable trade in opium with China and in indigo with Britain, and

---

[8] Shaking the pagoda tree was a colloquial term for white men making easy and quick money, often rapaciously, from native rulers and landowners, in the early days of Company rule in India. The pagoda was a gold coin used in the Madras Presidency up to 1818.

[9] Blair B. Kling, *Partner in Empire: Dwarkanath Tagore and the Age of Enterprise in Eastern India*, University of California Press, 1976, p. 54.

[10] William Jardine (1784–1843), who founded the business, was the largest smuggler of Bihar and Malwa opium to China via Canton, initially in partnership with Jamsetjee Jeejeebhoy (1783–1859) who became India's First Baronet of the Realm.

Gillanders, Arbuthnot & Company, which was started as a partnership by F.M. Gillanders and G.C. Arbuthnot. The other agency houses that soon became known as the major Calcutta-based British managing agencies entered in the late 1850s and 1860s. These had less to do with the export–import trade of their precursors, and got into India-based businesses. The best known among them were Mackinnon, Mackenzie in inland and coastal shipping, Bird & Company in coal and labour contracting for railway lines, and Andrew Yule & Company in zamindari interests and collieries. However, these firms, and some others, soon realized that there was much more to be gained by promoting new ventures and managing them for shareholders than by remaining as commission-based agency houses.

That, in essence, was the fundamental distinction between agency houses and managing agencies. The former ran sundry businesses as partnerships purely based on agency commissions. The latter went far beyond that by becoming the venture capitalists of the late nineteenth and early twentieth centuries, starting a slew of relatively modern enterprises that often required sizeable fixed capital outlays, offering shares in these enterprises to a wide body of native Indian and expatriate investors, securing profitable contracts to manage these businesses and creating appropriate organizational structures to oversee a wide horizontal portfolio of both interlocking and dissimilar businesses.

This book is about these business houses: the managing agencies that were the organizational core and

drivers of industrial growth in India from the last quarter
of the nineteenth century right up to their legislative
demise in 1970.

The Chapters

Strangely enough, the first real managing agency in the sense
that I have described it was not set up by the British. It was
Carr, Tagore & Company, formed on 1 August 1834 by an
amazingly multi-faceted businessman called Dwarkanath
Tagore (1794–1846), the most illustrious member of
the Jorasanko branch of the Tagore family until his pre-
eminence was bested by his grandson Rabindranath.

The story of Dwarkanath, particularly the span
and scope of Carr, Tagore & Company, which set the
contours of the modern managing agency, forms the
core of Chapter 2. It is a fascinating tale and shows how,
even at the height of British power in the region, an
urbane, canny, polyglot native Indian could play a hugely
important commercial and social role. It also highlights
Dwarkanath's colossal failures; how these put paid to
further growth of local entrepreneurship in eastern India
and instead led to the unfettered growth of companies
controlled by English and Scottish managing agencies.
The chapter ends with how this situation continued until
the entry of a young, confident and supremely determined
trader-cum-businessman called Ghanshyam Das (G.D.)
Birla in the early 1920s.

Chapter 3 focuses on corporate growth between 1875
and 1947 in India. Throughout this period most, if not

all, listed and unlisted public limited companies that came into being across India were promoted and controlled by managing agencies. Regardless of whether the companies were run by British or Indian entrepreneurs, managing agencies were the preferred instrument and form of corporate control. With some differences.

Up to the Great Depression of 1929–1935, the corporate world of eastern India covering the Bengal Presidency and Assam was overwhelmingly dominated by the English and the Scots. Many reasons have been posited. Ignoring the de rigueur fecklessness of wealthy Bengali babus and their congenital inability to be involved in the world of commerce, there is a more plausible explanation. Most of the goods produced in east India, such as gunny bags, burlap and tea, were exported to markets that were far more familiar to the rulers than to the ruled. This was not so in the Bombay Presidency. Here the dominant industry was cotton yarn and textiles. Despite some exports to China and later to Japan, the bulk of saleable yarn found its way to the local handloom markets, and cloth was produced entirely for domestic consumption. Here, the comparative advantage of knowledge and trade connections lay with the native businessmen. Add to that the innate trading and entrepreneurial ability of the Parsis, Gujaratis, Marwaris, Bhatias, Dawoodi Bohras and Kutchi Memons, it was but natural for industrialization in western India to be dominated by Indians.[11]

[11] One might offer yet another reason. The Bombay Presidency had a more egalitarian distribution of land, rural wealth and

The growth of Indian-controlled businesses was not limited to Bombay and Ahmedabad. Chapter 3 shows how local entrepreneurship came into play even in the British-dominated corporate world of east India from the mid 1920s, but more so in the 1930s and 1940s. This was not without serious resistance from the Anglo-Saxon incumbents. Yet, led by G.D. Birla, and followed by Sarupchand Hukumchand, Ramdutt Ramkissendas, Soorajmull Nagarmull, Bangur, Kanoria, Amritlal Ojha, Onkarmull Jatia, Sukhlal Karnani, Jaipurias, Karam Chand Thapar and others, Indians determinedly got into jute and coal. For Birla, it epitomized economic nationalism and swaraj. For other Indians who were using their managing agencies to control companies in hitherto British enclaves, it was far more prosaic—that of making the best of an opportunity whose time had come.

Elsewhere too, the Indian presence became more visible in the corporate world, such as in Kanpur with the advent of Kamlapat Singhania, who founded the JK group; or the anglophile Sir Jwala Prasad (J.P.) Srivastava who, after working as an industrial chemist for the United Provinces government, began to own dyeing plants, textile mills and other businesses in Kanpur (earlier Cawnpore),

---

trading networks before and after the ryotwari settlements under the East India Company. A greater egalitarian ecosystem, both economic and social, spawned a larger number of potentially risk-taking entrepreneurs than did the sharply pyramidal zamindari system of eastern India. It is a hypothesis worth testing.

Rampur, Bhopal and Gwalior; or Lala Shri Ram, who rapidly rose from being a clerk at the Delhi Cloth Mill to becoming its promoter; or the audacious Ramkrishna Dalmia, a Marwari from Rohtak who, having made an early fortune from speculation and trading, started a clutch of sugar mills throughout Bihar and the United Provinces and then aggressively moved into cement, setting up factories in Bihar, Sind, Punjab and the Madras Presidency. Almost everywhere, Indians were coming out of the woodwork to start various industries—and they invariably used the structure of the managing agency to control their businesses. It was a period of incredibly exciting churn, one that deserves description and analysis.

Chapter 4 looks at the developments from the time of Independence till the formal legislative demise of the managing agency on 3 April 1970. However, while the legal form of the managing agency was explicitly abolished by the insertion of section 324A in the Companies Act, 1956, its substance lived on in various forms, allowing entrepreneurs and promoter groups to exercise control over corporate cash flows that were appreciably greater than their equity stakes. But I am running ahead of myself.

In 1944, a group of Indian industrialists and economists published the Bombay Plan, which made a case for a 'mixed economy'—one in which the state and private industrialists would be equal partners in progress. Despite its coherent and fact-based arguments, the Bombay Plan's vision did not quite come to bear. Since the 1930s, Nehru was innately suspicious of capitalists and convinced of the need for socialism, a commitment that only strengthened over time. After the assassination of Mahatma Gandhi in January 1948, the death of Vallabhbhai Patel in December 1950, the self-appointed exile of Chakravarti Rajagopalachari to Madras and the elevation of Rajendra Prasad to the constitutional position of President of India, there were no senior centrist or right-wing leaders who had the stature to restrain Nehru. Not surprisingly then, independent India saw the growth of state-led socialism. It began with the Industries (Development and Regulation) Act 1951, which sanctified wartime licencing and controls in a time of peace. This was followed by the Industrial Policy Resolution of 1956, which stated that the future development of seventeen key industries (or Schedule A industries) would be under the exclusive domain of the state; and that of twelve others (Schedule B), while not barred to the private sector, would see progressively greater government participation. This 'commanding heights' resolution was buttressed by the second Five Year Plan that made a case for growth to be driven by Soviet-style heavy industrialization led by significant public investment for setting up giant state-owned enterprises. The era of commands, controls and government ownership of the means of production had begun.

While the tenor of these developments was markedly different from that of the 'partnership of equals' as suggested in the Bombay Plan, it did not significantly constrain the growth of private enterprise or the managing agencies. In truth, only a few of the business groups of the time had the financial strength and risk-taking ability to set up seriously large-scale enterprises such as the industries in Schedule A would have called for. Even some of the Schedule B industries such as aluminium, ferro-alloys, machine tools and fertilizers were beyond the ken of most. Thus, India travelled along a dual track of industrial growth, with major integrated steel mills and heavy engineering and electrical plants being set up as central government enterprises. Simultaneously, industries like jute, tea, coal, cotton textiles, cement, sugar and lighting continued to grow as did medium engineering units under the ownership and control of private entrepreneurs, where managing agencies still ruled the roost.

However, the writing was on the wall. Some of the major Indian entrepreneurial groups such as the Birlas, Tatas, Mafatlals, Kirloskars, Mahindras and Thapars began to understand that having one or two managing agencies directing an increasing number of legally distinct companies across a widening spectrum of industries and businesses was not the best way of exercising control. With the advent of government-sponsored financial institutions such as the Industrial Finance Corporation of India (IFCI) in 1948, the Industrial Credit and Investment Corporation of India (ICICI) in 1955 and the Industrial Development Bank of India (IDBI) in 1964, each set up to provide large loans for industrialization at affordable rates and tenor, long-term finance became more readily available. Attractive term loans helped finance larger industrial ventures with relatively modest equity contributions. This intervention reduced the pressure on promoters and their managing agencies to garner additional risk capital to finance new avenues of growth, while allowing them to continue to maintain corporate control over far larger enterprises in which they had low share ownership. This they could so long as they enjoyed a good working relationship with the term lending institutions.[12]

In this new world of accommodative development finance, which soon become integral to India's industrial growth in the 1960s, 1970s and 1980s, entrepreneurial groups no longer needed to construct complex arrangements using the managing agency system. Thus, as the scale of industrial entities grew in independent India, it became clear that the time-honoured form of attracting risk capital and maintaining corporate control, so well performed by the managing agencies since the late nineteenth century, was no longer necessary. Left to itself, the system would have withered on the vine.

---

[12] To appreciate this, consider a new company setting up a project worth Rs 900 crore. If it was entirely financed by equity and the promoter group wished to control the business by holding 20 per cent, it had put up Rs 180 crore. If, instead, the project was structured with a debt-equity ratio of 2:1 and all the debt was advanced by long-term loans from development finance institutions such as IFCI, ICICI and IDBI with generous terms and gentle covenants, then the promoters only needed to put in Rs 60 crore, i.e. 20 per cent of the equity component of Rs 300 crore. Therefore, if the entrepreneur paid his debt dues on time and remained in the good books of the term loan financier, he would have set up a large enterprise with low equity outlay while retaining control over vastly greater cash flows.

But other factors came into play to accelerate its demise, notably the Mundhra case, the Dalmia episode—which involved a series of tax evasions and shady inter-corporate transactions by managing agencies—and the growth of multinationals (MNCs) in independent India. The Mundhra case involved a hitherto unknown Calcutta-based Marwari trader called Haridas Mundhra, who used the profits from tea exports during World War II and thereafter to buy up sufficient shares of a series of British-controlled companies in the first half of the 1950s, both on his own account and also through a syndicate of other Indian businessmen. In each instance of buying, he would pledge the shares so purchased with banks to obtain additional finance for more such acquisitions. It was a Ponzi, made worse when Mundhra 'persuaded' the government-owned Life Insurance Corporation of India to purchase shares in half a dozen of his financially troubled companies. Soon the banks were overloaded with these stocks, many of which were found to be forged share certificates. A headline-making crisis erupted when Mundhra could not service the loans. Newspaper editorials wrote reams on the greed of rapacious traders now pretending to be industrialists. An investigation was launched and Mundhra was arrested. And, after a commission of inquiry, the finance minister T.T. Krishnamachari was forced to resign. Prime Minister Nehru went through the ignominy of being hauled over coals in Parliament by none other than his son-in-law, Feroze Gandhi.

The Mundhra episode allowed the English and vernacular press alike to tar and feather a cross section of Indian industrialists and their managing agencies, especially those controlled by the Marwaris. But it was nothing in scale compared with the Dalmia scandal. Various firms controlled by Ramkrishna Dalmia, who had been one of the fastest growing industrialists from the 1930s onwards, were accused of financial manipulations, tax evasion and illegal transfer of funds in favour of Dalmia's son-in-law Shanti Prasad Jain. All this was carried out through a system of interlocking companies via the group's managing agency Dalmia Sahu Jain & Company. The aim was to siphon money from listed companies into private entities. Although the report of a commission of inquiry could not conclusively prove straightforward and illegal diversion of funds, it became clear that such scams were devised, orchestrated and sustained through the managing agency system. It was the era of the 'temples of modern India', and Dalmia Sahu's business practices caused so much revulsion among the intelligentsia and the political class that it began to spell the end of managing agencies.

The third factor was the growth of MNCs. Though some of them had set up business relations with British managing agencies to get an initial 'feel' of the country in the pre-Independence era, such arrangements came to an end by the late 1950s and early 1960s. The MNCs had their own style of operations, and having soon mastered their knowledge of markets and logistics, they found no need whatsoever to form alliances with the fading lights of colonial enterprise.

If one were to add to a fourth factor—the innate hatred that Indira Gandhi had for private enterprise in general and the managing agency in particular—it was clear that the days of the managing agency were numbered. And so the curtain fell. It came down in two stages. In 1967, under powers given to the central government in section 324 of the Companies Act, 1956, the managing agency system was to be terminated in five industries by 1970. These were jute, cotton, sugar, cement and paper. Then section 324A was promulgated, which decreed total abolition of all managing agencies as of 3 April 1970. On the face of it, therefore, the structure that was started by Dwarkanath Tagore in 1834 and one that fashioned the growth of corporate India right up to the 1960s, came to a formal end.

But did it? That is the substance of Chapter 5, which argues that even in the absence of managing agencies, there were various legal structures and loopholes that allowed entrepreneurial groups—Indians and MNCs—to exercise disproportionate control over 'their' listed companies. It happened in many ways; and some of the more important ones, which now go by the rubric of 'related party transactions', are listed out in the chapter. Chapter 5 also shows that the essence of the managing agency was not unique to colonial or early independent India. In varying forms, but significantly similar in content, arrangements to confer disproportionate control and unequal cash flow rights vis-à-vis actual share ownership was evident throughout Asia across much of the twentieth century—in the structure of the *zaibatsus* and *keiretsu*s in Japan, the *chaebols* of South Korea, and among the latter day business giants of Hong Kong, Indonesia and the Philippines.

Why was this so? The answer lies in the commonality of two major factors in these geographies: relatively scarce supply of large risk-taking entrepreneurial groups in these countries and a high degree of concentration of banks and financial institutions. When the two coupled, as these did in Japan, South Korea and much of south-east and east Asia, the inevitable outcome was the growth of major business groups engaged in many diverse enterprises, all controlled by a series of private holding companies that exercised enormous power over their corporations and their cash flows.

In India, where managing agencies were formally abolished forty-five years ago, their essence still survives— and *will*, until India sees far greater democratization of the entrepreneurial spirit and access to risk and debt capital. At one level, that is beginning to happen. Led by the software majors and followed by professionally run private sector banks, mortgage finance companies, pharmaceutical entities, some of the automobile companies and consumer goods firms and, most recently, the IT services, 'app' and e-commerce firms, companies have consciously opted for sound corporate practices and good governance. Equally, there remain many companies—even among the top 100 listed ones, especially those that have many unlisted entities under their wing—which still engage in managing agency-like business practices that give the controlling entrepreneurial groups access to greater cash flows than what might have been possible in a more transparent and democratic corporate milieu.

On balance, I prefer to believe that we are changing for the better—at least in board and corporate governance practices across some of the large listed companies. But such change, though clearly happening, is not widespread enough. One hopes this too will happen, as has so much between the onset of economic liberalization in 1991 and the present day. It is a faith worth keeping.

2

THE KING OF CALCUTTA

St George's Hotel, London, evening of Saturday, 1 August 1846.

Amidst a terrific summer thunderstorm of the kind that the city had not witnessed in years, an immensely wealthy fifty-two-year-old Indian and loyal subject of the Crown breathed his last. Despite being a brahmin-turned-Brahmo, he was buried without any religious rites at the Kensal Green cemetery, watched over by his son, nephew, some friends and a few former business partners. The simple yet elegant tombstone, no more than a few feet tall, can still be seen. Its head carries this bare inscription: 'Dwarkanauth Tagore of Calcutta, Obiit 1st August 1846'. On the top of the tombstone are two letters, 'D.T.'[13]

---

[13] Unless otherwise stated, much of this chapter is from the classic work on what was probably the earliest managing agency in India: Blair B. Kling, *Partner in Empire: Dwarkanath Tagore and the Age of Enterprise in Eastern India*, University of California Press, 1976;

The story of managing agencies in India must necessarily begin with the many businesses of this incredibly enterprising man. Born in 1794, just a year after Lord Cornwallis as the Governor General of the East India Company had settled land revenues of Bengal under the Permanent Settlement, Dwarkanath was in every way to the manor born. Belonging to the Jorasanko branch of the Tagore family, he was not only born to great wealth, owning rent-yielding estates throughout east Bengal, but also to a family of the educated and cultured. Fluency in English, Bengali, Persian and Sanskrit was passé; the Tagore family home was in equal measure European and Bengali. The family was totally familiar with the British ways of doing business and enjoyed recognition as respected middlemen in the world of plantations, up-country trade, moneylending and even insurance.

Progress for Dwarkanath was an equal combination of three parts: meticulously accumulating wealth through trade, moneylending and commerce; pursuing Western social modernity; and simultaneously maintaining respect for all that was good in tradition. Thus, while nowhere close to being a radical like Rammohun Roy, twenty-two years his senior, Dwarkanath was absolute in his conviction to make sati illegal, which

and an earlier abridged version, 'The Origin of the Managing Agency System in India', *Journal of Asian Studies*, University of California Press, XXVI(1), November 1969, reprinted in Rajat K. Ray (ed.), *Entrepreneurship and Industry in India, 1800–1947*, Delhi, Oxford University Press, 1992, pp. 83–98.

Lord William Bentinck as Governor General did in 1829. Equally, he never stopped short of getting into serious clashes with the English to protect his business interests. Dwarkanath was as much a hard-nosed businessman as he was a modernist, and perfectly comfortable in both worlds.

By 1834, when he was forty, Dwarkanath was a seriously rich man with significant interests in land, indigo, opium, revenue collection and moneylending. He owned an opulently furnished mansion in Belgatchia, north Calcutta, from where he showered bountiful hospitality on Europeans and Indians alike. Recognized by the British as a Bengali babu worthy of respect, he was first made a *sheristadar* or Indian agent of the Company's salt monopoly in the 24 Parganas in 1822, and then, six years later, conferred the office of the Dewan on the Board of Customs, Salt and Opium, one of the highest public posts a native could possibly strive for. In addition, he was made a justice of peace. For Dwarkanath, it was time to up the ante.

In the mid-1830s Calcutta was the most significant city of British India. It was hardly splendid, what with its unpaved roads, the Black Town, heat, mosquitoes, fever and pestilence. But it epitomized growth, was the pivot that linked European trade and commerce with the wealth of the lower Gangetic plains, and a magnet to anyone seeking to make a fortune. With a population of around 450,000, the mainstay of Calcutta and its suburbs was foreign trade. The port on the Hooghly exported indigo and fine handloom cottons to Europe and huge amounts

of Ghazipur opium to Canton in China, the latter being
traded for Chinese tea, which was then auctioned off
in London to create a lucrative means of repatriating
wealth accumulated by British traders and ex-East India
Company men.[14]

On 1 August 1834, Dwarkanath resigned as the
Dewan, and started a completely new enterprise. It was
Carr, Tagore & Company, which would be the first and,
in its time, by far the most widespread and profitable
managing agency in Bengal.

Carr, Tagore & Company

Agency houses preceded Carr, Tagore & Company. In
essence, an agency house was an unlimited liability
partnership between two or more businessmen, typically
British, to engage in various import and export opportunities
that Bengal offered during the time. While the number
of agency houses had increased from between fifteen and
twenty in the last decade of the eighteenth century to
over sixty in 1834, most of them were small businesses
that did only one type of trade and, as partnerships, were
severely limited by their sparse capital. Only a few had
the necessary funds and the business acumen to engage
in multiple money-making opportunities that Bengal
offered to a risk taker in the 1830s.

---

[14] See Peter Marshall, *East Indian Fortunes: The British in Bengal
in the Eighteenth Century*, Oxford, Clarendon Press, 1976 and
Peter Ward Fay, *The Opium War, 1840–42*, University of North
Carolina Press, 1975.

Dwarkanath was certainly one such. Limited neither by finance nor commercial shrewdness, nor business appetite nor imagination, he was quick to realize that if an agency house promoted and then acquired control of a joint stock limited liability company, it could offer streams of income to the *promoting* entity without the risk of unlimited liability falling upon it in the event of a major default of the *promoted* company. For a native Indian to appreciate this in the colonial context of the 1830s was significant in itself. Dwarkanath's genius went further: he put money into the venture.

Soon after launching Carr, Tagore & Company in partnership with an indigo merchant William Carr, Dwarkanath wrote a fascinating letter to Governor General Lord William Bentinck stating that his new enterprise was based on a vision where it would be 'upon at par with, if not in advance of, the first houses of Calcutta . . . combining . . . the advantages . . . of European and native integrity, wealth and experience' to open up 'the productive energies of the country.'[15] His grand visions notwithstanding, Dwarkanath was canny too. While keeping the equity capital of Carr, Tagore & Company modest, he loaned the firm Rs 10 lakh from his own finances, which was registered as a debt carrying an interest rate of 8 per cent per year. In one stroke, Dwarkanath had provided the firm the requisite capital for expansion by way of creating new ventures, and had also guaranteed that he would be paid a healthy annual interest for this largesse.

[15] Kling (1976), p. 72.

Between the firm's incorporation in 1834 and its dissolution in 1848, sixteen months after Dwarkanath's death, Carr, Tagore & Company had eight partners, excluding the two founders. All but Dwarkanath were British, which probably reflected the founder's innate comfort in dealing with sahibs as well as his ingenuity in realizing that having white men as partners was an advantageous way of reducing racially motivated commercial risks. It also helped Dwarkanath to elevate his image from that of a rich zamindar–bania to one of a progressive 'merchant'. Of his eight partners, the most innovative was William Prinsep, more about whom will be written later.[16]

Partners came and went. But with Dwarkanath being the only continuing figure from 1834 until his death in 1846, there never was a question as to who was the real entrepreneur and decision maker. The firm's bread and butter business was export trade—in indigo, silk, sugar, saltpetre, hides and rice. Had it been just that, Carr, Tagore & Company would have been condemned to historical anonymity. But it was not, because Dwarkanath had other ideas.

[16] A brother of William's, James Prinsep (1799–1840), after being the assay master in the Calcutta and Benares mints, became famous for his works on numismatics, deciphering the Kharosthi and Brahmi scripts of ancient India and being the founding editor of the *Journal of the Asiatic Society of Bengal*. Lost at sea in 1840, he remains a part of today's Kolkata because of the Prinsep Ghat and its beautiful Palladian porch on the banks of the Hooghly opposite Fort William.

Coal, Steam tugs, Salt and Chain Ferries

The Raniganj mine in the district of Burdwan, some 130 miles north-west of Calcutta, possessed the richest proven coal seam in India. Various prospectors had operated it since 1815, and while there was no dearth of coal reserves, none could make profits. In 1834 and again in 1835, offers were made to sell the mine. When the mine was put up for sale the third time in July 1836, Carr, Tagore & Company bought it for Rs 70,000. Suddenly, the game changed for the firm.

By this time, Bengal was experiencing a sharp rise in demand for coal. With the steady growth in exports, both to Britain and China, more ocean going steamships were berthing at Calcutta; steamboats were now plying up and down the Hooghly and the Ganga right up to Allahabad; and eastward between Calcutta, Khulna, Narainganj and Dacca. Despite persistent problems in recruiting and training a workforce of diligent miners, especially Santhals, who felt that they had pleasanter things to do, the business of mining at depths of less than 100 feet with picks and crowbars and having buckets of coal being winched up by simple pulleys was hardly complicated. The cost of producing coal at Raniganj was minimal: around 3 pice per *maund* (or 82.24 pounds). The problem—the one that had wrecked previous enterprises—lay in transporting it in bulk at a cost that would make it attractive for the users and profitable for the producers. That solution needed more than picks, shovels, buckets, ropes, underpaid tribal labour and crude steam pumps for bilging out rainwater after the monsoons.

It was all about logistics. Raniganj coal mattered not a whit at the pithead, but everything if it could be economically transported to the places that needed it most. Making money involved reliably shipping the coal in sufficient bulk down to Calcutta and also up-river to Katwa, Murshidabad, Farakka and then on the Ganga to Rajmahal, Patna and Benares. That needed flat-bottomed steamers and tugboats.

Dwarkanath immediately got on with the job. Within months of his purchasing the Raniganj colliery, Carr, Tagore & Company bought a 120-horsepower paddle-wheeler steamboat called the *Forbes* at a debtors' auction for a princely sum of Rs 110,000. After spending a total of Rs 180,000 on the colliery and the boat within a short span of time, Dwarkanath realized that the coal logistics business needed consolidating. No prevaricator, he quickly invited a group of eminent businessmen to start a unique corporate enterprise, the Calcutta Steam Tug Association.

Structured as a joint stock association, the organization had a paid-up capital of Rs 200,000, comprising 200 shares of Rs 1,000 each. The shares were not freely transferable—once bought they could not be sold without the approval of the majority of shareholders resident in Calcutta. The first two purchases were steamboats: the *Forbes,* repurchased from Carr, Tagore & Company for Rs 120,000 and another, for Rs 80,000. The Calcutta Steam Tug Association had five directors who were elected annually, who appointed a secretary to conduct its day-to-day business. Dwarkanath's genius lay in not only getting Carr, Tagore & Company's money back by reselling the *Forbes*, that too at a profit of Rs 10,000, but also in ensuring his firm's appointment as the secretary of the Association for a commission of 5 per cent of net profits. Thus, Carr, Tagore & Company became India's first managing agency. As Kling points out:

> The new association was a landmark in the development of business organization in India. As a joint-stock company managed by a single agency house, the arrangement contained all the features of the managing-agency system . . . By combining the joint-stock form with agency-house management Tagore spread the risks of the enterprise while maintaining managerial control.[17]

The Calcutta Steam Tug Association had sufficient capital. Starting with Rs 200,000 in 1836, it soon doubled its equity capital base to Rs 400,000 in 1838, and then to Rs 500,000 in 1842. Between 1836 and 1844, it had five tugboats in service. It charged Rs 400 per day for tugging and another Rs 250 per day for return hire. After paying Carr, Tagore & Company its annual 5 per cent on net profits, the Association earned enough to declare dividends twice a year.

During 1836–44, total dividends per share announced by the Association amounted to Rs 1,390. There was, however, a rider. In 1848, two years after Dwarkanath's death, it was found that thanks to some lax accounting the value of the Association's assets was Rs 300,000 and

[17] Kling (1976), p. 125.

not Rs 754,000, as reported to the shareholders by the secretary of the Association. Hence, 500 shares of Rs 1,000 each, amounting to Rs 500,000 of paid-up equity, were impaired, with the asset value per share falling to Rs 600. Even so, an original shareholder in the Association had made money over twelve years—netting Rs 990 over the period at an average rate of 8.25 per cent per year. It was an excellent return on investment.[18]

Thanks to the Association's tugboats, Carr, Tagore & Company soon became the largest purveyor of coal across Bengal. By 1837, Raniganj was producing and supplying over 720,000 maunds of coal, or over 70 per cent of what was mined in Burdwan. By 1842, the Company's production and despatch had increased to a million maunds. Two years later, it had risen further to 1.38 million maunds; and by 1846 had exceeded 1.5 million maunds.

It was a hugely profitable business. At an average price of 5 annas per maund in Calcutta, Carr, Tagore & Company earned a revenue of Rs 312,500 by shipping a million maunds of coal in 1842. That year, the total cost of mining, rents, land taxes, Indian wages, European salaries, transportation, boat hire and storage at the various riverside depots was estimated at Rs 175,000. The profits amounted to Rs 137,500, or 44 per cent of revenue. To put it differently, at that rate of output, the company had recouped its initial investment of Rs 70,000 in a little over six months of sales!

At the rate of 7 annas per maund, as was the rate in the second half of the 1840s, profits soared to above

---

[18] Calculated from the data given in Kling (1976), p. 127.

Rs 260,000 per year. The halcyon years coincided with the Opium War (1840–42), when the government orders for Burdwan coal for steamships going to Canton and other Chinese ports significantly increased. Prices soared to over 12 annas per maund. Dwarkanath and his partners sang their way to the bank.[19]

As if this wasn't enough for Carr, Tagore & Company to manage the colliery and the steam tug business, it also got into salt pans. The brainchild of George Prinsep, a brother of Dwarkanath's third partner William, the project was to manufacture salt on industrial scale with the best available technology. George's experiments failed time and again. After his death in 1849, the firm, called the Bengal Salt Company, was taken over by his brother William, by then a partner in Carr, Tagore & Company. William first made Carr, Tagore & Company the managing agency of the Bengal Salt Company and then did everything he could to resuscitate the enterprise. However, it all came to naught, with the firm's last salt works in South 24 Parganas failing for one reason or the other—inappropriate technology, poorly constructed salt pans, damage by cyclones and gale force winds in the monsoons. Eventually the business was shut down, and Carr, Tagore & Company ceased to have anything to do with it; it had probably made no money from being the managing agent.[20]

[19] *Ibid.*, pp. 105–06, p. 113.
[20] *Ibid.*, pp. 131–35. Kling has an interesting observation to make. Because of the inability of Prinsep and Carr, Tagore & Company to make a success of this business, there was no modern indigenous industry to get into the breach when the

Prinsep and Dwarkanath were excited by another idea, this a revolutionary, game-changing one. By the 1830s, some 12,000 people were crossing the Hooghly twice each day between Howrah and Calcutta in small boats, and hundreds died when these capsized. How much safer, and how wonderfully lucrative, would it be to have a ferry bridge? The concept was simple enough and already in use in parts of England, involving a steam-powered ferry moving between two fixed points on either side of a river, anchored to and moving along powerful underwater chains.

For the Hooghly, it would be a floating iron bridge, ninety feet by ninety, pulled by two giant underwater chains fixed to both shores and operated by a powerful steam engine. Designed to make each crossing in seven minutes, it was supposed to transport over 1,000 people per trip. The revenues from 12,000 daily foot passengers at half a pice each, and from cabin passengers, palanquins, buggies and carriages, were estimated at Rs 60,000 per year, versus an operating cost of Rs 24,000. The net profit of Rs 36,000 per annum would suffice to recoup the estimated capital cost of Rs 177,000 in less than five years.

Dwarkanath soon floated an enterprise called the Steam Ferry Bridge Company with an initial issue worth Rs 200,000 consisting of 2,000 shares of Rs 100 each, and with Carr, Tagore & Company as the managing agent. Wealthy citizens of Calcutta were convinced of the venture's sure-shot

---

government's salt monopoly ended in 1863, and India was then swamped by English salt.

success, and the flotation was excitedly oversubscribed.[21] Unfortunately for Dwarkanath, this grand project was riddled with problems—delays, cost hikes and various unforeseen exigencies. Within a year of incorporation, the project cost had burgeoned by 51 per cent, from Rs 177,000 to Rs 280,000. Matters worsened a year later. Costs rose yet again, and for the project to be completed each shareholder needed to put in another Rs 100 per share. A group of livid investors demanded a special meeting to debate whether the firm should be liquidated.

In the meantime, the two ferry bridges arrived, but in different ships. The machinery of one was in good condition but that of the other, hauled from London in the hold of a leaky vessel, had rusted beyond redemption. By now, liquidation had become a *fait accompli*. A shareholders' meeting in August 1842 decided exactly that, confirming that all the machinery had to be sold— which it was for Rs 80,000. That, then, was the second failure of Carr, Tagore & Company. Calcutta had to wait for thirty-two years for its first pontoon bridge across the Hooghly, costing £220,000, and another sixty-nine years for the iconic, cantilevered Howrah Bridge.

And So to Tea

Little might a person sipping a cup of strongly brewed Assam tea today appreciate how much is owed to Dwarkanath, William Prinsep and Carr, Tagore &

[21] *Ibid.*, pp. 138–9.

Company for their key roles in founding the industry that brought Assam tea to the world. In 1837, an enterprising government set up the first experimental tea garden in upper Assam, which gradually replaced Chinese tea with the local variety and then started sending small shipments to London for tasting and inspection. The word was out that tea could be cultivated in India.

Three London businesses then approached the East India Company for permission to grow tea in Assam. Soon enough, one of the three, representing powerful East India merchants, formed the Assam Company, with a plan to raise share capital of £500,000 consisting of 10,000 shares of £50 each, of which a fifth or 2,000 shares would be reserved exclusively for Indian investors. The steps for actual flotation had begun when the Assam Company suddenly came to know that a local, Calcutta-based enterprise had also got into the act. It was the Bengal Tea Association, a joint stock enterprise with an estimated capital of Rs 10 lakh under the managing agency of Carr, Tagore & Company.[22]

This was Dwarkanath and Prinsep at their tactical best. Dwarkanath had got wind of the move in London and tried to pre-empt it by setting up a competing enterprise in Calcutta, which he believed was better suited to seek favours from the local government. Prinsep wrote to George Eden, first Earl of Auckland and Governor General at the time, asking for his support. Auckland sought a more detailed proposal from the promoters, which Prinsep

[22] *Ibid.*, p. 145.

sent to him and to the secretary to the Government of India. Realizing that doing this alone would be financially stressful for Carr, Tagore & Company, and dreading that such a move might lead to strong opposition from the British-based Assam Company, Prinsep kept the collaborative door open by suggesting that, if needed, further capital could be raised 'by a corresponding association in England'.[23]

It was a great ploy. Reluctant to get into disputes with entrenched Calcutta interests, the Assam Company approached Prinsep to arrange what it called a 'junction of interests'. London accepted Prinsep's condition that directing the affairs of the plantation be the preserve of Calcutta, and that none of the 2,000 shares sold in India could be repurchased in London. In exchange, Prinsep agreed that the Bengal Tea Association be called the Bengal branch of the sterling-based Assam Company, and that the local affairs be managed by Carr, Tagore & Company. That settled, May 1939 saw the shareholders of the soon-to-be erstwhile Bengal Tea Association resolve to 'form a junction' with the Assam Company, with a *proviso* that local management of this unique, double-headed company with two boards of directors would be conducted by directors elected exclusively in India under the managing agency of Carr, Tagore & Company.

While tactically admirable, it was an intrinsically unworkable arrangement. After serving as a secretary to the Indian branch of the Assam Company in its first year and as its local chairman for another sixteen months,

[23] *Ibid.*, p. 146.

Prinsep resigned in November 1841 and left India for Britain in June 1842. After his departure, the relationship between London and Calcutta rapidly deteriorated, with the former determined to not only call the shots but also to minimize the role of Carr, Tagore & Company in Assam Company.

That was but inevitable. With control over merely 500-odd shares out of 10,000, Dwarkanath's managing agency could only speak for 5 per cent of the equity, which was hardly enough to exercise disproportionate managerial rights. By the mid 1840s, control of the Assam Company decisively shifted to London. It had to because it was London, not Calcutta, that had supplied the capital to cover the losses of the first decade of operations. On paper, the two boards continued up to 1866, with the Calcutta board working in an increasingly desultory manner, powerlessly sulking at each instance of greater control by London. That year, this peculiar case of fiduciary diarchy came to an end. London abolished the Calcutta board and instead appointed Calcutta-based European firm Kilburn & Company as its managing agent. Carr, Tagore & Company suspended its business on 31 December 1847, sixteen months after Dwarkanath breathed his last. The Assam Company continued as a prosperous sterling enterprise for several decades after India's independence, until it was first acquired by a Marwari firm and later by a Bermuda-based non-resident Indian. In addition to tea, it now exports shrimp, tuna, fish meal, rice extractions and soya meal.

Rise and Fall of the Union Bank, 1829 to 1847

Growth in mercantile business and exports, especially of indigo in the pre-chemical dye days, needed large-scale, organized funding. Not surprisingly, the financier in Dwarkanath realized the need to set up a new, well capitalized bank. In 1929, he and the partners of Mackintosh & Company unveiled a project to form a joint stock bank with an authorized capital of Rs 5 million, comprising 2,000 ordinary shares of Rs 2,500 each. By September 1929, with Rs 1.2 million already paid up, the Union Bank opened its doors for business.[24]

Unfortunately, neither Dwarkanath nor the shareholders nor the management appreciated a fundamental dictum of any bank—that it must spread its risks across a portfolio of different types of loans. From its inception, the Union Bank relied almost exclusively on the financing of a single exportable, indigo, a commodity that was grown and processed by financially irresponsible, often dissolute, up-country planters and subject to the vicissitudes of major price fluctuations. Within a year of its launching, the bank faced its first crisis when an uncollateralized loan of Rs 600,000—or half of its paid-up capital—went sour. It took three years and huge efforts for the bank to weather this storm. Matters improved from 1833, and the bank started declaring modest dividends.

However, amidst a brief period of prosperity, Dwarkanath and the directors made some decisions that

[24] *Ibid.*, p. 199.

were to stretch the bank's resources to the hilt. They raised the bank's capital from Rs 1.5 million to Rs 10 million in four instalments; decided to go the whole hog in financing the production of indigo; and simultaneously to dramatically extend the bank's presence in bill discounting.

There were fundamental contradictions between the two approaches to lending. Bill discounting earned small returns per transaction, needed large amounts of readily available circulating capital, but was an essentially safe business; whereas indigo plantation loans, while earning potentially greater returns, were inherently risky fixed investments, which locked up significant capital for relatively long periods. The two could only be done together with a substantially large loan book. Soon, resources were stretched, as were the returns. Dwarkanath and his partners had built a financial juggernaut on very weak operational foundations. It needed a set of shocks for the house to come crumbling down.

The shocks began in 1840, when indigo prices began their steep and secular decline. Instead of cutting its losses and focusing more on the safer bill discounting business, the Union Bank kept upping its stakes in indigo. Bad loans were not written down but supported by further loans; books were falsified; unviable indigo plantation mortgages were refinanced; and with every passing month the bank kept losing money—both interest income and capital—while claiming that it was in profits. Eventually the management was forced to admit that it had lost over Rs 2.4 million in financing the production of indigo, an estimate that hid more than it revealed.[25] Then followed a huge commercial crisis in Britain, which completely shut off indigo exports and accelerated the bank's decline to insolvency. In January 1846, the Union Bank suspended all its businesses. A year later, it was liquidated.

Dwarkanath was dead and gone by then. In his last year, he was sharp enough to realize that the Union Bank was heading towards bankruptcy. In 1845, therefore, he cut his losses and sold most of his Union Bank shares. It is difficult to determine whether this unwinding was only on account of his insight that the bank would fail; or whether it also reflected his desire to convert his share ownership across various business organizations into cash and plough this into his zamindaris for the benefit of his dependent sons, none of whom, including Debendranath Tagore—father of Rabindranath—had the slightest desire or capability of running any corporate venture. For all these considered actions, it is difficult not to pin some blame on Dwarkanath for the eventual collapse of an institution that could have been a symbol of financial success. By virtue of his significant stock ownership and disproportionate voice in the commercial affairs of Calcutta, Dwarkanath had forced the bank to take appreciably more business risks than was warranted by its capital. He also overlooked mismanagement, instances of financial laxity and fraud by the senior, white officials. It was as if the idea of a venture was enough and execution didn't seem to matter.

[25] *Ibid.*, pp. 213–14.

A Character, Indeed

How does one evaluate a multi-faceted, larger-than-life character like Dwarkanath Tagore, a babu who, in a land conquered by the British, could design, create and finance the basic framework of a corporate system that continued for over 150 years? It was not for nothing that he was called a Raja by the Indian community and even 'Prince Dwarkanath' by some Europeans, for he lived a life of royalty. From the mid-1820s, and right up to his death in August 1846, he was not just the wealthiest businessman and corporate entrepreneur but by far the leading public person of Calcutta.

For him, philanthropy, pomp, parties, polemics and grand displays, all of which he threw himself into with abandon, served a uniform purpose—that of asserting the parity of high-class Indians like himself with the highest of the British residents of Calcutta. Committed to scores of Hindu charities, Dwarkanath was one of very few natives who donated in equal if not greater measure to Western causes. His desire to be at the top of the philanthropy pool was so intense that he would make sure he donated Rs 50 or Rs 100 more than the next best in the pecking order.[26]

---

[26] The donations spanned various charities: a huge amount of Rs 100,000 to establish the Dwarkanath Fund for the Needy Blind; large regular donations to the Native Fever Hospital which later became the School of Tropical Medicine of the Calcutta Medical College; for the widows of the Afghan War; and far from home, for the Irish destitute after the potato famine.

He was also the king of soirees, invitations to which were as precious as those of the Governor General's. Dwarkanath's parties at the Belgatchia estate were major social events, attended by the Governor General and hundreds of other guests, including all the European and Eurasian female beauties of Calcutta. One dance followed another; crystal glasses remained filled with wine, port or brandy; the evenings ran into late nights and ended with a huge display of fireworks. Though a Europhile, Dwarkanath was just as generous in throwing parties for fellow Indians—in a very different setting, but with just as much alcohol accompanied by all the worthy nautch girls of the city.

He patronized Western theatre, his love for which was no less than his desire for the company of Western women. Dwarkanath, it was said, could charm and secure the affections of almost any lady he liked, and did not in the least bother to conceal his affairs with European women, be it in Calcutta or during his two long trips to London. Equally, he was a vocal advocate of universal female education which, unfortunately, he failed to see in his lifetime.

The comfort his persona generated in people who made his acquaintance and his ability to socialize with the highest strata of Europeans extended far beyond the municipal limits of Calcutta. During his first trip to England in 1842, Dwarkanath met, among others, Robert Peel, the prime minister; the Lord Mayor of London; the Duke of Wellington; the Duchess of Kent; and Prince Albert and Queen Victoria, who liked him sufficiently to invite him to two events, one of which was a private dinner. On his second trip in 1845, the one from which he never returned, Dwarkanath again met the Queen and Price Albert, conversed with William Gladstone on the possible admission of Indians to Parliament, threw a literary party for Charles Dickens and William Makepeace Thackeray, and wenched and dined out almost every day. One cannot think of a single Indian of the time, or indeed right up to the second quarter of the twentieth century, who could socialize so freely and speak his mind with the highest and most powerful among the imperial rulers of the land. His was an amazing tour de force.

In the more prosaic world of trade, commerce and industry, Dwarkanath was a great success with some severe limitations. Other than being a successful zamindar, moneylender, and an indigo and opium trader, he played a direct role in either founding or fostering five major businesses in eastern India: collieries through the Raniganj company; steam tugs via the Calcutta Steam Tug Association; salt production through the Bengal Salt Company; tea under the Assam Company; and banking through the setting up of the Union Bank in 1929, which became the largest commercial bank of the region until it collapsed in 1847. To this one should add his managing agency's revolutionary foray into ferry bridges, which failed to see the light of day.

If one were to dissect these enterprises, it is obvious that two—coal and steam tugs—were spectacular successes, and became so under the control of Carr, Tagore & Company. Another eventually succeeded more than all the others; it was the Assam Company, but its success had little to do with the entrepreneurial drive of either Dwarkanath or his favourite English protégé William Prinsep. And three failed: salt, the Steam Ferry Bridge Company and the Union Bank, with the last failure causing considerable financial pain to Dwarkanath and his family since the bank was not protected by limited liability. On the positive side, he was doubtlessly an innovator who, in effect, visualized, created and executed the managing agency system, which was to continue right up to the early 1970s and, thereafter, in various forms up to the present day.

Yet Dwarkanath was too much of a restless entrepreneur. The meticulousness with which he had looked after his zamindaris and the opium, indigo and other exports in his early years gave way to the adrenaline rush of conceiving new enterprises and in being the richest, best connected and most powerful English-, Bengali- and Persian-speaking native that Bengal had ever seen. Clearly, his forte lay in creating enterprises; he seemed to have far less interest in efficiently managing them. Each business that failed did so because of poor oversight and execution, wrong choice of managers, and an occasional turning of the Nelson's eye to financial irregularities. For these mistakes, Dwarkanath was as guilty as his partners in Carr, Tagore & Company.

Herein lay the contradiction. On the one hand, Carr, Tagore & Company created the basic framework of the managing agency system, which would continue for well over 150 years. And, at his best, when Dwarkanath was a totally focused businessman, the firm was truly brilliant. Yet, on the other hand, he often failed to give the companies that he pioneered the managerial skill sets they badly needed. Delighted as he was in their promotion and in designing clever agency contracts for them, he became increasingly averse to the tedium of sustained, day-to-day execution.

The outcome was tragic. While Dwarkanath died a hero and Carr, Tagore & Company holds a special place in the economic history of business organizations in India, shareholders of that era, native Indians and Europeans alike, grew to shun the Indian managing agency. Native entrepreneurs were seen as too risky to be involved with. In that vacuum created in east India, the British took over, and did so with a vengeance from the last quarter of the nineteenth century onwards, until they were challenged by Indians in the inter-war years. The challenge was made first gingerly and then with an increased conviction that came from success. Yet, in the final analysis, if Dwarkanath were alive today, wouldn't he smile and immodestly say, 'Didn't I show you so?'

3

1875–1947: 'YEAR AFTER YEAR OUR TRADE INCREASES'

Uttered with great pride by a Scottish chairman of the Indian Jute Mills Association (IJMA), this exultation best expresses the growth of Indian industry from the last quarter of the nineteenth century until the end of the 1920s, and then from the mid 1930s till 1947. There was much truth to this rejoicing. Between 1875 and up to the beginning of World War I, Great Britain, India's largest trading partner, grew like never before. As Chart A shows, Britain's real GDP increased at an astoundingly exponential trend rate of 1.8 per cent per annum over thirty-eight consecutive years, almost doubling from £94 billion in 1875 to £182 billion in 1913. In an era of agriculture and manufacturing, with no buoyant service sector to speak of, it seemed a time of neverending boom, fed by imports of food, raw material and myriad primary products, and

51

driven by rapidly growing exports of a great variety of
manufactured goods.

Chart A: Real GDP of Great Britain (£ billion)

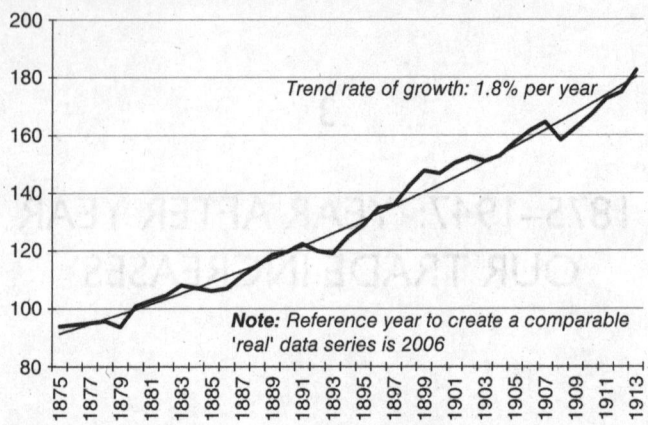

Trend rate of growth: 1.8% per year

Note: *Reference year to create a comparable
'real' data series is 2006*

Source: *Bank of England,* Three Centuries of Data

Between 1875 and 1913, real imports into Britain
increased over 2.7 times, growing at an annual trend rate
of 2.6 per cent. Exports from the country grew at the same
rate. It was the trade-driven British Empire at its most
glorious. As Eric Hobsbawm noted in *The Age of Empire,
1875–1914*, this was the time of the internal combustion
engine that needed both oil and rubber; the time when
over 100,000 railway locomotives were pulling over 2.75
million carriages and wagons across the world in long
trains spouting banners of smoke such as one in which
Joseph Mallord William Turner sat one stormy afternoon
to paint his magnificent *Rain, Steam and Speed—The
Great Western Railway*; the time of enormous growth
in use of iron ore, copper, tin and nickel; the time of

great gold demand to protect and bolster expanding trade through a global currency fully backed by the precious metal; the time when grain and meat were imported in huge quantities for a growing working class population across Britain; and the time for copious tea drinking by the British, whose per capita consumption rose from 1.5 lbs in the 1840s to 5.7 lbs by the 1890s. Britain's imports of tea rose from 40 million lbs in the 1840s to 224 million in the 1890s.[27] Small wonder then that the chairman of IJMA was euphoric: the world needed more and more gunny bags for wool, cotton, wheat and saltpetre, and gunny cloth for wrapping beef shipped from Argentina to Britain. The Age of Empire was the Age of Business.

India of the time was impoverished by any standard, and would remain so right up to its independence and even later. George Nathaniel Curzon, imperial pro-consul extraordinaire at the turn of the twentieth century and Viceroy of India from 1899 to 1905—he of Eton and Balliol College—grandly proclaimed his territory to be 'the brightest jewel in the British Crown', and prosperous at Rs 30 per capita (£2) per year in 1901–02.[28]

[27] Eric Hobsbawm, *The Age of Empire, 1875–1914*, Vintage Books, 1989.

[28] A very clever, ambitious and immensely opinionated Conservative, Curzon was much disliked by some in Balliol who came up with a nasty doggerel 'My name is George Nathaniel Curzon / I am a most superior person. / My cheeks are pink, my hair is sleek, / I dine at Blenheim once a week', which stuck through his life.

Curzon's number was an underestimate. Careful work by S. Sivasubramonian shows that per capita GDP in 1901–02 was Rs 47 at current prices, and Rs 59 at constant 1938–39 prices.[29] Despite Curzon's assertion of India's per capita GDP being 57 per cent lower than Sivasubramonian's, the fact was that India was a plodding, miserably poor country and would remain so right up to Independence and beyond.

During the first forty-seven years of the twentieth century, India's real GDP grew—if one were to use such a term at all—at 1 per cent per year, and in per capita terms by a pathetic 0.25 per cent. The problem was the primary sector, dominated by agriculture, whose share in GDP was as high as 60 per cent in 1900–01. Over the period, it grew at a niggardly rate of 0.4 per cent per annum, which is another way of saying that it did not grow at all.[30] Not surprisingly, the dominant picture of the countryside under colonial rule was one of parched earth, hunger, desperately thin men and women in ragged clothes and emaciated cattle.

Yet, for all the poverty of the Indian masses, the British raj had put in place institutions to ensure that India could move ahead with trade, commerce and manufacturing. On 16 April 1853, barely two decades after the introduction of the railway in Britain, a fourteen-carriage train drawn by three locomotives embarked on India's first railway

[29] S. Sivasubramonian, *The National Income of India in the Twentieth Century*, New Delhi, Oxford University Press, 2000, henceforth Sivasubramonian (2000), Tables 6.9 and 6.10.

[30] *Ibid.*, Table 6.10.

journey from Bombay to Thana, a distance of twenty-one miles that took about forty-five minutes. The company that started it was the Great Indian Peninsular Railways, among whose ten directors were Sir Jamsetjee Jeejeebhoy and Jagannath (Nana) Shunkerseth. After the 1857 uprising, there was greater urgency to invest in railways so that troops could be rapidly transported to anywhere in the country in the event of another revolt. The Calcutta–Allahabad–Delhi line opened for business in 1864; the Allahabad–Jabalpore branch line in 1867; and the Bombay–Calcutta line via Allahabad in 1870.[31] By 1875, some £100 million were invested by British companies in Indian-guaranteed railways. By 1880, the network route was around 9,000 miles, mostly linking the major port cities of Bombay, Calcutta and Madras to the interiors. Goods, both manufactured imports and raw material from the hinterland, could therefore be quite easily and safely transported to their destinations.

Then there were the banks. Despite the spectacular collapse and liquidation of the Union Bank of Calcutta in 1847, corporate India was reasonably served by a banking network that was at least as good as those in other peripheral nations of the British empire. There were the three Presidency banks—Bank of Bengal, Bank of

[31] This is the one that Phileas Fogg and Passepartout travelled in Jules Verne's *Around the World in Eighty Days*. They needlessly broke journey to ride an elephant through forests for 50 miles for the line was complete in all respect. The positive was an action-packed chapter and a dramatic rescue of the beautiful Aouda from sati.

Bombay and Bank of Madras—that were brought under an identical format by the Presidency Banks Act (Act XI) of 1876. Between 1876 and 1914, non-government deposits of the three banks rose significantly: ten-fold from Rs 20 million to Rs 201 million in Bengal; eleven-fold from Rs 9 million to Rs 99 million in Bombay; and twelve-fold from Rs 7 million to Rs 87 million in Madras. Over the same period, the banks' loans, overdrafts and bill discounting business grew from Rs 31 million to Rs 106 million in Bengal; from Rs 18 million to Rs 70 million in Bombay; and from Rs 7 million to Rs 75 million in Madras.[32]

There were other banks too. Allahabad Bank was established in 1865; Hong Kong and Shanghai Bank opened its offices in Calcutta in 1869; Oudh Commercial Bank was set up in Faizabad in 1881; and Punjab National Bank in Lahore in 1894. By the early twentieth century, several other banks came up, and they remain up to this day. Three were set up in 1906: Bank of India in Bombay, Corporation Bank in Udupi and Canara Bank in Mangalore. Bank of Baroda came into being in 1908 under the aegis of the Gaekwads. And Sir Sorabji Pochkanawala helped establish Central Bank of India in 1911, which was entirely Indian-owned and managed. More banks followed in the 1920s and 1930s. While these banks as a rule did not offer term loans for setting up companies or purchasing machinery, the more reputed managing

[32] Amiya K. Bagchi, *The Presidency Banks and the Indian Economy, 1876–1914*, Calcutta, Oxford University Press, 1989, Tables 3.1 and 3.2, pp. 119–120.

agencies and their firms had sufficient access to them for bill discounting and working capital.

In 1875, the Bombay Stock Exchange was established, the second oldest in Asia after Tokyo. The Ahmedabad Stock Exchange followed in 1894, and then the Calcutta Stock Exchange in 1908. Establishment of these three regulated bourses ended an earlier anomaly between entrepreneurs and managing agents, who could secure their capital from banks, and individual shareholders, who had no recourse to an organized exchange for trading their shares. Thus, in large measure, corporate ownership now became divisible and transparently tradable.

All the necessities for rapid corporate growth were in place: banks and indigenous moneylenders for credit; ports for import and export; railways for inland transportation; and stock exchanges for corporate valuation and trade in securities. Moreover, despite the racial bias of the white man against the babus, local lawyers, pleaders and obsequiously jabbering natives who were especially ubiquitous in Calcutta, commercial and corporate laws from the mid-Victorian era were by and large fair, without any distinctive or persistent preference in favour of the ruling class. In fact, from the early twentieth century, records often show a healthy disrespect that many colonial civil servants had for the British *boxwallah*s and a more-than-occasional unwillingness to bend rules for their benefit. These factors, representing an amazing coming together of institutions needed for corporate development, allow for a bold hypothesis. It is this: no colony under any empire lying between the Tropics of

Cancer and Capricorn was better prepared for corporate growth than India.

Entrepreneurs, both British and native Indian, responded to these factors. As Chart B shows, modern, factory-sector manufacturing grew at 3.7 per cent per year, increasing its share from just about 2 per cent of GDP in 1900–01 to cross 10 per cent by 1945–46. How the British—and later, Indian managing agencies—played the game in this era is the story to which I now turn.

Chart B: GDP from factory manufacturing, 1938–39 prices

Source: Sivasubramonian (2000), Table 6.10

PART I: 1875–1929

British Managing Agencies of Calcutta—The Early Years

Just as the expansion of the British empire in India followed no premeditated, grand imperial design, so too was the pattern of progress of managing agencies of Calcutta. These grew in response to a remarkably rapid and sustained growth in hitherto unknown business opportunities such as manufacture and export of gunny bags and cloth, creation of plantations for a burgeoning tea drinking population in Britain and the rest of Europe, and mining coal for railways, factories and the new steam-based world of shipping. All these activities required commercial enterprise; and in a country limited by entrepreneurial talent, these ventures were best created and controlled by a few who had the resourcefulness and sufficiently deep pockets—all channelled through the conduit of managing agencies.

After the liquidation of Carr, Tagore & Company, Calcutta saw no more Indian managing agencies till the arrival of Birla Brothers in 1920. From the late 1840s to 1920, the managing agencies of the city were exclusively British. How did they come into being? As briefly touched upon in Chapter 1, a few of the larger mercantilist agency houses that existed prior to 1850, particularly Gillanders Arbuthnot & Company and Jardine Skinner, transformed themselves into managing agencies as they expanded in scale and areas of business.

Gillanders Arbuthnot, oldest of the major managing agencies of Calcutta, was first established as an agency house in 1819 by Captain F.M. Gillanders to import general merchandise and piece goods from Liverpool and Glasgow, and export indigo from India. The firm remained as a purely mercantile agency house right up to 1870, and then got involved in industries and plantations when it began to take shares in lieu of repayment of trade advances that had gone sour, principally in the declining indigo business. From 1870 onwards, under the stewardship of H.N. Gladstone, a son of William Gladstone (four times prime minister of Britain under Queen Victoria), the firm began to expand and diversify. It entered the tea business as garden agents, and soon became the managing agent for three jute mills: Balliaghatta in 1872, the Hooghly Mills in 1883, and the Gondalpara Mills in 1895 which was located in the French-administered territory of Chandernagore up the Hooghly, twenty-two miles north of Calcutta.[33]

Jardine Skinner was formed as partnership in Bombay in 1844 between David Jardine, who was related to the managing partners of the great Hong Kong company Jardine Matheson, and John Skinner, a prosperous opium merchant, born and brought up in India and related to James Skinner of the famous regiment Skinner's Horse. Soon enough, Jardine Skinner opened its agency house in Calcutta and, until the advent of jute manufacturing, traded mostly in opium, after which it became the managing agent of four jute mill companies in Bengal.[34]

Unlike Gillanders, Arbuthnot and Jardine Skinner, which were mercantilist agency houses that turned into full-fledged managing agencies controlling various manufacturing and trading businesses, many of the newer entrants after the 1850s came to Calcutta as

[33] Jones (1992), pp. 5–6.
[34] *Ibid.*, p. 12.

managing agencies to promote a slew of India-based enterprises. Notable among them were Andrew Yule, Bird, Mackinnon, Mackenzie & Company and Macneill & Barry. There will be more about Andrew Yule and Bird later in the chapter. For now, it is useful to outline a brief history of the other two.

In 1856, a Scotsman called William Mackinnon founded Calcutta & Burmah Steam Navigation Company and secured a contract from the postal service to carry mail between Calcutta and Rangoon. This then became British India Steam Navigation Company, which was incorporated in London with a paid-up capital of £35,000 to build a fleet of steamers and serve the Indian coasts, the Persian Gulf and Singapore. Mackinnon Mackenzie subscribed to 20 per cent of its shares for £7,000, becoming the firm's agent. In 1862, it publicly floated British India Steam Navigation in London, increased the paid-up capital to £400,000 and continued as the managing agent. By the last quarter of the nineteenth century, British India Steam Navigation was by far the most important, powerful and monopolistic shipping company; and with the Suez Canal being opened in 1869, it created a very profitable line between India and Britain.[35] After the death of Sir William Mackinnon,[36] there being no heirs to the enterprise, the managing agency was acquired by the

---

[35] This monopoly was temporarily challenged in the 1920s by Walchand Hirachand's Scindia Steam Navigation Company, more of which is examined later in this chapter.
[36] The original partner, Robert Mackenzie, drowned in a shipwreck in 1852.

Inchcape family. James Mackay, later Lord Inchcape, one of the most tough and hard-nosed Scottish businessmen of the colonial era, not only merged the steamship company with the larger P&O line but also expanded into other businesses such as jute and inland transport.

The managing agency of Macneill & Barry was the amalgam of two Calcutta-based partnership firms: Barry & Company and Macneill & Company. Later, a third firm came into the fold. This was Kilburn & Company, one that secured the agency of Assam Company after Carr, Tagore & Company. Given that one of the founders, Dr J.B. Barry, was a doctor in an Assam tea garden, the initial interests of this managing agency was in tea. But it soon diversified into jute manufacturing and set up the Bengal Jute Mill and took over two others, Ganges and Gourepore. Over time, Macneill & Barry came under the control of James Mackay and the Inchcape group. In its heydays, the managing agency controlled several ventures including two major inland river steam navigation companies that shipped raw jute from east Bengal to the mills in Calcutta, a large number of tea gardens in Assam, several collieries, two insurance companies, India's largest rope manufacturing unit called Ganges Rope, and later, light engineering units under the supervision of the Kilburn arm.[37]

---

[37] Incidentally, this managing agency also helped set up the Calcutta Electric Supply Company Limited which, now under the control of Sanjiv Goenka, is still the sole supplier of electricity for the megalopolis and its surroundings. See Jones (1992), pp. 29–30.

Common to all British managing agencies that came into being in the second half of the nineteenth century and expanded thereafter until the Great Depression of the 1930s was their focus on business opportunities largely within eastern India and less on the traditional export–import trade of the agency houses of yore. Initially small in size, many of them expanded enormously with the boom in jute manufacturing, tea plantations and collieries that started from the mid-1870s and continued unabated till the end of 1929.

What were their structure and common features? If there was a shared theme running across all major managing agencies in India—whether run by the British, Parsis, Marwaris, Khatris, Gujarati banias, Armenians, Bohras, Kutchi Memons, Chettiars, Kama Naidus or Tamil brahmins—it was that all of them focused on *horizontal control* of many enterprises across different, often unrelated, industries and trades. Horizontal control sharply contrasts with growth through vertical integration, where a firm incorporates, lists, controls and runs the businesses of a major industry through forward and backward linkages across the entire production and value chain. Examples of such firms are John D. Rockefeller's Standard Oil Company, which dominated the US oil industry, or Krupp of Essen in Germany, which ran Europe's greatest iron and steel conglomerate and then went up the value chain to manufacture steel-based arms and ammunition, or Reliance Industries across the entire petrochemical chain in today's India. As will be evident in Chapter 5, horizontal control was also the leitmotif of large business conglomerates in Japan (zaibatsus and keiretsus), in Korea (chaebols), in Hong Kong, Mexico, Brazil, Philippines and many other parts of the world.

There are two plausible explanations for the managing agency's emphasis on horizontal control. First, in a region that offered numerous profit-making opportunities, none requiring significant technical or managerial skills, that was also bereft of enough entrepreneurs with sufficient capital at their command, the relatively few that got into industry found it worth their while to enter as many lines of business as they could. Simply put, why stick to jute when you could also run collieries, set up tea plantations, put up sugar mills, manage small railway operations and organize inland steamer companies? The second reason was risk aversion. If you vertically controlled an entire industry or business chain and it went through a major slump, you could be ruined. However, if you ran distinctly different businesses, the downturn in one could well be countered by continuing profits in some of the others.

Were the agencies partnerships or privately held companies? In the early years, up until the second decade of the twentieth century, most managing agencies were organized as unlimited liability partnership firms having offices in Britain and in Calcutta, with the senior partners working out of home, and the juniors having to prove their mettle in Calcutta. The number of partners varied between five and fifteen depending upon the number of businesses these managing agencies handled as well as the span of the companies under their control. From the 1920s, and more so in the 1930s, most of the partnerships in Calcutta morphed into privately held limited liability companies because such a legal status protected the erstwhile partners from being personally liable for large, unforeseen losses. The corresponding British firms tended to remain as partnerships because the losses, if any, were entirely absorbed by the first line of defence—the limited liability managing agencies in Calcutta—while the repatriated profits were there to be shared by the partners in Britain.

Were agency partners men of family extract or were they outsiders? For most British managing agencies up to the end of World War I, the partners, in the case of both the UK and Calcutta firms, came from the families of the promoters, and were their sons, cousins, nephews or sons-in-law. Most of them were from Scotland, and some from England.[38] That changed in Calcutta after the war. The scale and span of business of these managing agencies expanded at a rate much faster than the supply of morally sound and commercially reliable relatives. Soon enough, each of these firms had to hire outsiders—mostly Scots but also Englishmen from known or extended families—as covenanted assistants and ship them out to India to run coal fields, jute mills, steamships and the tea business. By the early 1920s, recruits were also sought from those with a public school or grammar school education.

[38] Thus, the early partners of major British managing agencies such as Jardine Skinner, Andrew Yule, Gillanders, Arbuthnot and Mackinnon Mackenzie were all Scottish. See Maria Misra, *Business, Race and Politics in British India c.1850–1960*, Oxford, Clarendon Press, 1999, hereafter Misra (1999), p. 2.

Nevertheless, family links and private recommendations remained important and, up to the end of World War II, almost all partners and many covenanted recruits could claim to be connected in some way or the other to the promoting families.[39]

Some of the covenanted employees excelled in the job; and those that did also absorbed the ethos, values and quirks of their managing agencies. They became 'insiders', and were often rewarded with partnerships or, in the limited liability company regime, with directorships of the managing agency and of the companies under its control. Typically, a covenanted assistant came to work in India in his early twenties; and if he was good enough, became a partner or director in his Calcutta firm in another fifteen or twenty years. After remaining as a Calcutta partner, managing or resident partner, director or managing director for another seven to eight years, he would return home to be either a partner in the British office or to take up paid directorships of several India-based sterling companies.[40] For the most part, however,

---

[39] Shaw Wallace was an exception in that it prohibited members from the families of partners to be employed in the firm, either in Calcutta or in London. *Ibid.*, p. 32.

[40] Among the 'outsider' covenanted assistants that came good were H.C. Bannerman of Macneill & Barry and Owain Jenkins of Balmer Lawrie. From a middle-class Dundee family, Bannerman was selected by the firm towards the end of World War I and sent to Calcutta on a four-year contract. He worked in the jute department and then diversified into tea and inland shipping. In 1940 he became a partner of the firm in Calcutta, which was followed by his becoming the senior resident (or managing)

the partners in the British agency offices continued to be dominated by members of the promoting family or by those that held the largest blocks of shares.

So far as the Indian managing agencies were concerned, be it in Bombay, Calcutta, Delhi, Kanpur or elsewhere, family ties were even more important. Right up to the formal demise of the managing agency in 1970 and even later, the people who controlled such firms and their promoted enterprises were almost universally from the extended family and trusted kin. This was true even for the more Westernized Parsi managing agencies such as those run by the Tatas and the Wadias.

How much did the managing agency employee or partner earn? In their first four-year contract, junior assistants typically started with Rs 400 per month, this rising to Rs 550 (roughly £350) a month in the fourth year plus an annual bonus of around 25 per cent—a very handsome pay for a young bachelor in Calcutta just after World War I. New covenants were negotiated every four to seven years, and salaries rose quite rapidly with each. At the end of each contract, the employee received

---

partner in 1947. After Macneill & Barry became a limited liability company in India in 1947, Bannerman became its chairman. He then returned home in 1950 to work as a partner in the London office and thereafter served as an executive director of the Inchcape Group. Owain Jenkins came from a different stock. The son of a senior ICS officer, Jenkins was educated at Charterhouse and Balliol College, Oxford. He joined Balmer Lawrie in 1929; worked in the firm's tea gardens; then rose from being the executive assistant to becoming the managing director in 1949. *Ibid.*, pp. 32–33 and Jones (1992), Appendix I.

a fully-paid-for return passage to Britain plus a holiday of three to six months at 50 per cent to 70 per cent of the pay. Senior assistants, typically those with a decade of service to show, would get a salary starting at around Rs 2,000 per month and rising to a princely sum of Rs 3,500 plus bonuses. When a man in his forties was selected as a partner, he was loaned money from the managing agency to buy his share in the firm, which was then set off against his share of profits. A person who rose from covenanted assistant to senior partner or managing partner in Calcutta could expect to return home in his early-to-mid-fifties with savings of £60,000 or more—a huge amount by the standards of the time and much more than any senior retiring officer of the Indian Civil Service or the army could take home.[41]

At the risk of oversimplification, the structure of the typical British managing agency house in the early twentieth century is given on the next page.

What were some of the distinctive features of managing agency contracts with the enterprises that they controlled? Other than charging healthy commissions on sales and profits, managing agencies in Calcutta, Bombay and elsewhere universally insisted upon several onerous conditions and demands, some of which were:

a)   That they be the sole managing agent of the business, an arrangement that could never be changed except with express consent of the managing agency.

---

[41] Misra (1999), pp. 34–35.

Location	Organization and Legal Form	Employees	Profits
In Britain	Managing agency run as a partnership	British	Repatriation of profits from the Calcutta managing agency
In Calcutta	Managing agency run either as a partnership or as a privately held limited liability company	All partners, directors and seniors were British; clerical staff were generally Bengalis and occasionally 'Madrasis'	Commission on sales; commission of profits; fixed payment for the secondment of the agency's British employees; other commissions depending upon interlocking trade arrangements with companies managed by the same agency; and share of distributable profits as dividends proportional to the managing agency's shareholdings in their firms
At the jute mills, tea gardens and collieries	Publicly held, generally listed, limited liability companies. Mostly rupee companies, though there were some large sterling firms in tea and jute	Board of directors appointed by the managing agency. Invariably 'white' with sufficient representation of the agency. The managers were British and always chosen by the managing agency. The supervisory and technical staff were British, a few of whom were appointed by the agency. The clerical employees were mostly Bengalis; and workers were Indians from Bihar, eastern UP and occasionally upper Assam	Net profits available for distribution as well as for various reserve funds including special ones such as 'Dividend Equalization Reserves'

b)   That neither the managed company nor its board
     of directors had the right to revoke the managing
     agency contract, unless approved by the agency.

c)   That all decisions regarding the organization and
     running of the company and its businesses be
     conducted by the managing agency, except only in
     instances where required otherwise by corporate
     law.

d)   That they be the sole selling and purchasing agent as
     well as the broker, shipping and landing agent of the
     company.

e)   That in the event of handing over the managing agency
     to another firm, the incumbent be compensated with
     up to twelve times their total commission by the new
     entrant.

f)   That in the event of the enterprise winding up, the
     managing agency would have priority over all other
     claimants.

To sum it up in one sentence, a managing agency's
power over the enterprises it controlled was total and
absolute.

Jute in Calcutta

Two far-off wars created huge international demand
for commercial crops from India. With the Union navy
blockading the Confederate ports of Savannah and
Charleston during the American Civil War (1861–65), the
mills of Lancashire were rudely deprived of the cotton

cultivated in Georgia, Alabama and South Carolina, and were forced to opt for the next best substitute, the crop grown in the black soil area of the Deccan. What started as a vast upsurge in raw cotton exports to Britain petered off after the war; and, over time, became the source of supply to the newly set up spinning and composite mills of Bombay and Ahmedabad.

Likewise, the Crimean War (1854–56), which abruptly cut off the supply of Russian flax that was shipped from Sevastopol and Odessa, forced the mills in Dundee to quickly look elsewhere for fibre to weave packaging cloth. The substitute that soon gained importance was jute, a crop cultivated in the damp heat of the riverine plains of east Bengal. It didn't take much prodding for packaging manufacturers to opt for the substitute at a time when world trade was growing at 5 per cent per year. By the 1860s the average export of raw jute from Calcutta to Dundee was over 2.6 million cwt. per year.[42]

Soon, the Scots began to appreciate that jute could be even more profitably spun and woven into gunny bags and cloth in and around Calcutta itself. For one, since jute was grown in the districts of east and north Bengal, the entire global supply of raw material was within easy reach. For another, power-driven spinning and weaving

[42] Or over 343,000 metric tons. Unless otherwise stated, references for this section flow from Omkar Goswami, *Industry, Trade and Peasant Society: The Jute Economy of Eastern India, 1900–1947*, Delhi, Oxford University Press, 1991, henceforth Goswami (1991).

techniques were simple and could just as well be picked up by native labour at wages substantially lower than in Dundee. Besides, Calcutta had a good port, and adequate barge facilities could be established to locate mills on the banks of the Hooghly. Finally, there were enough rich Bengalis, Marwaris, Armenians, Baghdadi Jews and others who were looking for avenues for investment. Having burnt their fingers with Carr, Tagore & Company and smaller trading firms, where better to invest than in 'sound' managing agencies run by the dependable ruling whites of the land?

The year 1855 saw the first jute mill founded by George Ackland at Rishra, on the right bank of the Hooghly north of Calcutta. By the end of 1875, there were eighteen jute mill companies along the river, with a total of 3,500 looms, all set up by British managing agencies. By 1900–01, Calcutta and its neighbourhood had thirty-five jute mills, with total paid-up capital of Rs 41 million for the rupee companies and £1.6 million for the sterling firms, and whose cumulative capacity was 315,000 spindles and 15,340 looms. These mills consumed over twelve million maunds of raw jute (approximately 448,000 metric tons) to produce around 447,000 metric tons of gunny bags and cloth valued at over Rs 140 million, of which over 90 per cent was sent overseas. They directly employed over 110,000 workers, mostly from Bihar and eastern United Provinces, and was a major source of livelihood for four million peasant families, not to mention thousands of middlemen from itinerant up-country raw jute traders who bought the fibre from the farms to the larger merchants who aggregated the crop and passed it on to Calcutta. Within twenty-five years, the industry had grown to become the second largest modern factory-based sector in colonial India, the country's most significant hard currency earner, and an essential to the economics of the Presidency of Bengal.

The jute industry of the time—as indeed the coal and tea industries—was exclusively controlled by British managing agencies. At the summit stood Andrew Yule & Company, which began in 1863 when Andrew Yule, a young Scottish entrepreneur, arrived in Calcutta to start a business in a country of vast promise. Between 1875 and 1893, the firm continued to expand under Andrew's elder brother George Yule, and was already looking after jute mills, tea, coal, zamindari interests and insurance.[43] Its truly spectacular growth, however, occurred under the founder's nephew David Yule (1858–1928), who joined the company in 1875 and soon became the managing partner in 1893 at the age of thirty-five. A kind yet extremely able workaholic, David Yule lived in a small bachelor's apartment above the office. By 1900–01, thanks to his perseverance and execution, Andrew Yule & Company controlled over thirty public limited companies in jute, coal, tea, railways and inland steamship navigation, plus a large, landed estate in the

---

[43] George Yule was also a leading public figure of the time—as the Sheriff of Calcutta in 1886 and the President of Indian National Congress in 1888.

district of Midnapore organized as a commercially viable zamindari enterprise.[44] Knighted in 1912, Sir David continued to expand the business into power, paper and engineering. At the advent of World War I, Andrew Yule & Company was by far the largest managing agency house in India, with thirty-seven companies under its control, among which were ten jute mills.[45]

The other major managing agency in jute and coal was Bird & Company, which started in 1864 when Captain Sam Bird, the Allahabad agent for India General Steam Navigation Company, secured a goods handling contract with East Indian Railway. More such contracts followed with other major inland shipping companies as well as with Eastern Bengal Railway. By the late 1870s, Captain Bird, now joined by his son Paul, started a sawmill and secured the agency for the

[44] Dwijendra Tripathi and Jyoti Jumani, *The Concise Oxford History of Indian Business*, Oxford University Press, 2007, henceforth Tripathi and Jumani (2007), p. 70.

[45] Sir David Yule retired in 1919 after converting the partnership with its associated goodwill to a private limited company called Andrew Yule & Company (Private) Limited. The shares of this company were then bought by the British subsidiary of the great American banking house J.P. Morgan, which persuaded Sir Thomas Catto (1879–1959) to be the executive chairman of the company in Calcutta from 1919 to 1929. After which Sir Thomas returned to London as a partner of an investment bank called Morgan, Grenfell & Company while remaining as a non-executive chairman of Andrew Yule & Company until 1939. Subsequently, he became the Governor of the Bank of England (1944–49).

Burrakur Coal Company. Then the firm floated the Indian Portland Cement Company and, in 1880, made its first foray into jute manufacturing by setting up the Union Jute Mill. 1881 saw a young Calcutta-born-and-educated Englishman called Ernest Cable (1859–1927) join the firm. He, more than anyone else, played a major role in a remarkable expansion of Bird & Company across a large number of businesses: coal and mica mining, coke manufacturing, brick making including fireclay bricks for furnaces, more jute mills, dock contracts and stevedoring, insurance, jute baling and gunny exporting, engineering, and several other enterprises. Knighted in 1906 and conferred a baronetcy in 1921, Cable's greatest coup was in 1917 when Bird & Company engineered the purchase of another Calcutta-based managing agency, F.W. Heilgers.[46] After Cable's death, the firm was led by his son-in-law Edward Charles (Tom) Benthall, another legendary figure in the history of the enterprise; Benthall also became a member of the Bengal Legislative Council, the Imperial Council of the Viceroy of India and, finally, a member of the Board of Governors of the Bank of England.[47] We shall see more of Benthall in a short while. As far as jute went, the Bird-Heilgers group was on a par with Andrew Yule & Company at its zenith, controlling ten jute mill companies.

[46] Jones (1992), pp. 36–38.
[47] His family's greatest legacy to business and economic historians is the bequest of all his official correspondence to the archives of the Centre for South Asian Studies, Cambridge.

Then came three other managing agencies: Jardine Skinner, Thomas Duff and McLeod. Together, they constituted the 'Big Five' in jute.

The power of these five managing agencies was enormous. In 1900–01, corporate concentration was not all that marked, with as many as seventeen managing agencies controlling thirty-five jute mill companies. That soon changed. Every subsequent burst of investment between 1901 and 1925 saw the Big Five expand and consolidate their position by growing looms, setting up new units and buying off existing mills. By the eve of World War I, the five controlled 60 per cent of the industry's weaving capacity.[48] Managing directors of mills under these agencies, or senior partners who looked after the jute business, held the chairmanship of the industry body, the IJMA, for thirty of the forty-seven years between 1900–01 and 1946–47.

The period 1900–1914 was one of rapid growth in global demand for primary products and, consequently, made for years of great fortune for the jute mills. For the six years leading up to 1914, the average net profits as a percentage of paid-up capital of the twenty-nine listed jute mill companies were: 17.6 per cent (1909); 14.5 per cent (1910); 10.8 per cent (1911); 31.7 per cent (1912); 40.5 per cent (1913); and 17.8 per cent (1914). In some

[48] In 1914, Bird controlled 20 per cent of the industry's looms, Jardine 15 per cent, Duff 11 per cent, Yule 9 per cent and McLeod 5 per cent. IJMA, *Report of the Committee 1914* (Calcutta, 1915), table on looms, quoted in Goswami (1991), p. 59.

years, as in 1912 and 1913, some of the mill companies were earning net profits that were well over 50 per cent of their paid-up capital. Great dividends were declared; the shareholders were delighted; and the managing agencies were taking even more as their share of sales and senior employment contracts. It was an era of unfettered profits and optimism.

Fortunately for the jute mills, World War I turned out to be an even more profitable time because the dirty, wet war was fought largely in trenches that needed millions of sand bags. In fact, the war was fortuitous in terms of both supply and demand. It led to a severe shortage of shipping space, which immediately affected the export of raw jute to Dundee and elsewhere and led to the bottom falling out of the market. Prices crashed from Rs10.6 per maund of raw jute in 1913–14 to Rs 5 in 1914–15; and while it marginally picked up in the next few years, it dropped yet again in 1917–18.

While costs fell dramatically, on the product side there was a killing to be made. In the very first year, there were government war orders for 50 million gunny bags per month. Between 1915 and 1918, the mills supplied 1.4 billion gunny bags, 713 million yards of gunny cloth, 5 million yards of jute canvas and a million pounds of twine as war orders from Britain, India, Australia and other Allied nations. In addition, the industry sold another 2 billion gunny bags and over 5 billion yards of cloth for commercial use to the allies and neutral countries, which is where it made money hand over fist. The profits were astronomical, as Table 1 shows.

Table 1: Net profit of jute mills as a share of their paid-up capital, 1909–18

Managing Agencies	No. of mills	1909–14	1915	1916	1917	1918
Andrew Yule	8	30%	77%	79%	51%	173%
Bird & Heilgers	10	22%	67%	100%	73%	147%
Jardine Skinner	4	18%	67%	98%	64%	220%
McLeod	3	18%	82%	101%	78%	156%
Begg, Dunlop	2	28%	78%	95%	76%	146%
Kettlewell Bullen	2	24%	85%	106%	64%	187%
George Henderson	1	24%	37%	57%	50%	63%
Gillanders, Arbuthnot	2	11%	47%	72%	41%	130%
Barry	1	12%	60%	62%	31%	156%
Average	**33 mills**	**23%**	**70%**	**91%**	**63%**	**162%**

Source: Investor's India Year Book (IIYB) 1919 (Calcutta, 1919), used in Goswami (1991), Table 4.3, pp. 94–5.

Dividends on ordinary shares ranged from a minimum of 100 per cent to as much as 330 per cent of the face value, with shares trading at eight to ten times their par values. Astounded by the frenzied bullishness of the times, Edward Benthall, soon to become the chairman and managing partner of Bird & Company, wrote in his diary:

> Flotations of every kind were proceeding apace . . .
> and the share of any flotation jumped to an immediate

premium. Partners, assistants and friends of the firm who were given allotments were able to sell at a profit and did so without delay . . . The general spirit of the times is illustrated by the head of a technical department who, when engaging a man, said, 'Don't worry about the pay, son. You can make far more on the Stock Exchange and any time you like you can walk across and double your salary.'[49]

Amidst this phenomenal prosperity in a spotlessly white corporate enclave, where gabardine-suited, sola-topied British could poke aside with their rattan canes the native Indians who were in their way as they walked the Chowringhee en route to Falettis for the traditional Saturday lunch,[50] seeds of conflict were being sown.

[49] Godfrey Harrison, *Bird and Company of Calcutta, 1864–1964*, Calcutta, 1964, pp. 133–34, quoted in Goswami (1991), p.96.

[50] The poking canes story was fondly recalled by J.A. Mckerrow, a partner of Bird & Company in his retirement speech. *Papers of Sir Edward Benthall* (henceforth the Benthall Papers), Box XIV, Centre for South Asian Studies, University of Cambridge. Those were, according to Mckerrow, 'the good old days'. For a young British covenanted employee in a managing agency, Calcutta was a great place to be. 'Sundays in Calcutta, especially in the cold weather, were a great deal of fun . . . The day began with a 6.30 a.m. service at the Cathedral, which we'd attend wearing jodhpurs. Then we'd pick up our horses and go around the jumps . . . Then we would do 18 holes of golf and have a swim, and have brunch. We would then go home to the chummery for a sleep, then to the Saturday Club to play squash, ending up with Evensong at the Cathedral and then going to the pictures.' William Tully (father of the Delhi-based journalist

Although British managing agencies ran the jute mills and much of the export trade in gunny bags and cloth, the Marwaris were very much in charge of the raw jute trade from east and north Bengal to the mills around Calcutta. They were also increasingly present as exporters of both raw and manufactured jute and had become significant enough to be members of the elite Calcutta Baled Jute Association (CBJA) affiliated, as the IJMA was, to the British-controlled Bengal Chamber of Commerce.[51]

Then there was *fatka* or speculation and hedging in raw jute and gunny. Started by six Marwari traders in 1905–06, fatka became wildly popular in the span of half a decade because the minimum unit of transaction was five bales, or twenty-five maunds. The original fatka bazaar at Afim Chowrasta behind the Writers' Building where once Ghazipur opium was auctioned by the Company to British, Parsi and other Indian merchants for shipping to Canton, was jammed from morning to night with speculators of all hue—'members of the Bar Library, tramway conductors, businessmen, babus and

---

and author Mark Tully), who worked for Gillanders, Arbuthnot & Company. Jones (1992), p. 12.

[51] Even as early as 1909, there were ninety-five Marwari members of the CBJA, comprising well over half of the membership, with names such as Ghanshyam Das Birla, Sarupchand Hukumchand, Surajmull Nagarmull and Ramdutt Ramkissendas who were soon to play a larger role in the industry. CBJA, *Report of the Committee 1908–09* (Calcutta, 1909), pp. 26–8, and Goswami (1991), p. 85.

bhistis'—each having a little flutter.[52] Soon fatka quotes were telegraphed to major raw jute buying stations in east Bengal. Long used to spot buying, the British mill owners tried what they could to get the government to put an end to fatka. The government did nothing, and for a long time the British remained confused about forwards trade and hedges while the Marwaris continued to dominate fatka, which became a permanent feature of both jute and gunny trade. Suddenly, for the acutely perceptive, there were many Marwari shadows at the edges of this 'whites only' business.

The first explicit change occurred after World War I. It had much to do with Ghanshyam Das (G.D.) Birla, a determined young man from Pilani in Rajasthan, who had migrated to Calcutta in 1911, all of seventeen, to join his elder brother Jugal Kishore in running the family business of brokerage, silver and opium trade and speculation. Birla soon started his own firm, which specialized in raw jute and gunny trade. By the end of World War I, it had done so well in jute and gunny broking as well as in fatka as to be among the top three in the business. In 1917, Birla even set up a London office run by Sonny Gubbay, an urbane Baghdadi Jew from Calcutta. By 1918, G.D.

[52] A contemporary civil servant wrote, 'The impression that will be made is not likely to be forgotten . . . Today every inch in every floor is occupied. The number of shops have increased to over one hundred and . . . accommodation is more valuable than in Threadneedle Street.' Government of Bengal, Commerce Department, Commerce Branch, File 2G/1, July 1916, Progs.212–215B, letter by E.A. Gubbay, undated.

was everywhere in the jute chain—purchasing raw jute, baling it, selling it to mills around Calcutta and in Europe, buying gunny bags and cloth and exporting these to the rest of the world. With one exception. He was not in manufacturing, and the huge wartime profits spurred his resolve to change that.[53]

After spending considerable time convincing Jugal Kishore to consider manufacturing, Birla decided it was time to set up his own jute mill. Bank support was difficult to come by, with Bank of Bengal initially refusing a loan, then agreeing only at a higher rate of interest. Promoted by the managing agency Birla Brothers, Birla Jute Manufacturing Company offered in its prospectus 250,000 ordinary shares of Rs 10 each plus 12,500 preference shares of Rs 100 each bearing 7.5 per cent interest. Eventually, however, only Rs 5 was called up per ordinary share, and Rs 50 per preference share, making for a total of Rs 18.75 lakh versus the original estimate of Rs 37.5 lakh. Not only was the enterprise under-funded but it also had to reckon with postwar escalation of machinery costs.

Besides, Birla faced severe opposition from the British managing agencies who were livid that an Indian mill could enter their domain. Andrew Yule & Company was particularly aggressive. It first grabbed the land that G.D. wanted for the factory and forced him to move to

[53] See Gita Piramal, *Business Legends*, Viking, 1998, henceforth Piramal (1998), pp.27–8; and Medha M. Kudaisya, *The Life and Times of G.D. Birla*, Oxford University Press, 2003, henceforth Kudaisya (2003), pp. 43–5.

Budge Budge, south of Calcutta; it then instructed its inland steamship company to charge extra freight for transporting raw jute to Birla's mill. At one point, things were so bleak that Birla thought of selling out and made a tentative offer to Andrew Yule & Company. When he arrived at the Yule office to negotiate a deal, a Scottish partner accosted Birla and gave him a talking-to for having the temerity to establish a jute mill. G.D. withdrew his offer and steeled his resolve to break the British monopoly in jute manufacturing.

Which he did. By 1920, he had set up Birla Jute with 392 looms under the managing agency of Birla Brothers of 7, Royal Exchange, Calcutta. Entering the fray with equal vigour was Sir Sarupchand Hukumchand, a noted Kasliwal Jain businessman from Indore, who established the Hukumchand Mill at Halishahar, north of Calcutta, under the managing agency of Sarupchand Hukumchand.[54]

Given the commercial prosperity of the post-World War I era, with the steady rise in looms, gunny output and exports, and average net profits clocking in excess of 20 per cent of paid-up capital, one might have thought that two jute mills under the control of Indians ought not have caused panic among the sahibs in the British managing agencies. But it did. Their key opponent was G.D. Birla, who was by now feared as a determined, blunt-talking, English-speaking Indian nationalist, far from the subservient bania that the British were so

[54] Kudaisya (2003), pp. 46–7.

used to. Besides, their fear that 'Indians are determined to get into *our* industry which will mean survival of the fittest in due course'[55] was becoming a reality. Seeing the profitable growth of Birla Jute and Hukumchand, other Indians too entered the business: Raigarh Mills in 1925; Gagalbhai Mills (started by a Gujarati entrepreneur Mafatlal Gagalbhai) and Juggilal Kamlapat Jute Mills in Kanpur (started by Kamlapat Singhania), both in 1927; followed by Adamjee Jute Mills (set up by Adamjee Hajee Dawood), Premchand Jute Mills (by Raja Janoki Nath Roy), Shree Hanuman and Shree Bajrang, all in 1929. Although the Indian mills accounted for no more than 6 per cent of total loom capacity and less than 8 per cent of total gunny output, they represented the thin end of the wedge—the desis in the goras' club.

There was a more subtle method by which Indians were creeping into this British preserve. This began in the early 1920s and became apparent only by the end of the 1930s. It involved important Marwari banias garnering enough shares of jute mills to demand or be offered seats on the boards of companies controlled by British managing agencies. How it occurred is a story worth telling.

On the strength of their reputation based on past performance, British managing agencies would float shares of new jute mill companies. Given their prestige and

---

[55] CSAS, Benthall Papers, Box I, marginal notation by Sir Edward Benthall, Mokandlall-Benthall, 3 December 1928, emphasis mine.

track record, these issues were invariably oversubscribed, which made it simple enough for any managing agency to control 'their' companies despite owning as little as 10 per cent of the stock because the vast majority of small shareholders—friends or otherwise—were only too glad to bequeath control rights to them for a steady stream of dividends. It was as if the managing agencies had perfected the art of controlling companies with minimum ownership. Thus, by the late 1920s, Andrew Yule & Company's shares in the mills that it controlled varied from a high of 43 per cent to a low of 7 per cent, but mostly ranged in the late teens and early twenties; the span of equity control of Bird-Heilgers ranged from 15 per cent to 23 per cent; for three of the four mills under Jardine Skinner, the managing agency's share ownership was 6 per cent, 13 per cent and 21 per cent; and in two of the four mill companies under McLeod, the agency owned just 1 per cent and 9 per cent.[56]

This strategy of controlling an enterprise despite low share ownership depended on the support of a large number of shareholders representing the 'uncommitted middle' which, in turn, hinged upon dividends. Unfortunately, dividends are poor instruments for maintaining perennial control over a large body of smaller shareholders. In difficult times, when dividends dip and share prices fall, many small investors choose to sell out instead of taking further losses. Equally, if a company does exceptionally well and declares greater-than-expected dividends, share

[56] Lokanathan (1935), p. 187.

prices tend to rise quickly, and some shareholders sell to make large capital gains. Maintaining corporate control with low ownership via dividends requires companies to declare exactly the 'expected' dividend each year so that few shareholders, if any, are induced, either from fear or greed, to sell out. This is very difficult in theory, and almost impossible to sustain in practice. In part, this is what happened throughout the 1920s, when friends of partners and company executives who were given shares, and some of the uncommitted 'middle', sold to book large profits. The buyers were Marwaris.

That was not all. Something far more significant was taking place in the 1920s that would intensify through the 1930s and 1940s. From the late nineteenth century, some Marwari families had developed close commercial relations with the British managing agencies, especially in the supply of raw jute and sale of gunny. For instance, the Jatias were banias of Andrew Yule & Company, with the patriarch Sir Onkarmull (1882–1938) being a close associate of David Yule; the Kanorias had a longstanding association with McLeod; Rameshwar Nathany with Jardine Skinner; and the Bajorias, Bangurs, Sohanlall Doodwawalla and Sir Badridas Goenka with Bird & Company.

During the inflationary 1920s, many jute mills, especially the ones that came up after the war, found themselves undercapitalized and often in urgent need of infusions of working capital. For example, Andrew Yule & Company's ten jute mill companies had an average capacity slightly under 700 looms, with average paid-up capital that was a bit above Rs 24 lakh, or less than Rs 3,500 per loom—hardly capitalized enough to run the business. Bird-Heilgers, also with ten mill companies, was just a shade better, with paid-up capital being not much more than Rs 4,000 per loom. For Jardine Skinner's four mill companies, paid-up capital per loom was under Rs 2,600; and for McLeod's four units, it was Rs 3,470.[57] There was no way that such grossly undercapitalized mills could have expanded production the way they did in the 1920s without recourse to other forms of finance.

But how and from where? Though available, bank finance was not enough because the banks of the time were conservative and not only demanded greater margin money but also undervalued the collateral of raw jute and gunny. Debentures and non-convertible preference shares were sometimes issued to meet financing needs, but these instruments were more expensive than bank loans. For most of the jute mills, the financing gap was often met by funds from cash-rich Marwari banias who had filled their coffers during World War I without the slightest pressure of having to declare large dividends for shareholders or partners, and who were now only too happy to oblige with loans at interest rates a percentage point or two below the going rate on debentures or preference shares. As collateral, they took shares of the jute mill companies that they loaned to, which had to be given out of the kitty of the British

[57] *IIYB*, successive issues.

managing agencies. Soon, some banias had enough shares to be invited to join the boards.[58]

Their entry was not insignificant. In 1918, only three of the 114 directorships of jute mill companies listed on the Calcutta Stock Exchange were held by Marwaris. By 1924, sixteen of the forty-six companies controlled by British managing agencies had at least one Marwari on their boards, with five having two Marwari directors. By 1930, 59 per cent of the jute mill companies controlled by British managing agencies had at least one Marwari director. The dhoti-clad, *pugree*d 'mugs with money' who earlier sat outside the accounts department to wheedle the Bengali clerks to pay their raw jute bills and who had to give way to the sahibs in the lifts were now beginning to sit in the wood-panelled boardrooms of the high-ceilinged offices in Dalhousie Square.

Expectedly, this influx triggered racial abuse. The Marwaris were 'pirates', 'outsiders', 'corner-boys of our great trade' and 'short-sighted industrialists' always 'up to some dirty work'. Although a member of the IJMA, Birla was often singled out as the villain of this 'native' piece—'acting bobbery [*sic*]' by doing 'more to encourage

---

[58] For details on this aspect of creeping Marwari control see Goswami (1991), Chapters 5 and 6; as well as Omkar Goswami, 'Collaboration and Conflict: Indian and European Capitalists and the Jute Economy of Bengal', *Indian Economic and Social History Review (IESHR)*, 19(2), pp. 141–79, 1982; and Omkar Goswami, '*Sahibs, Babus* and *Banias*: Changes in Industrial Control in Eastern India, 1918–1950', *The Journal of Asian Studies*, 48(2), pp. 289–309, 1989.

new mills than anyone'.[59] Even Sir Edward Benthall, the managing partner of Bird & Company, who was more careful with his words than other British boxwallahs, wanted 'to see one of the upstart mills going into liquidation . . . and coming back to British management, whoever it may be'.[60] That was not to be.

Meanwhile, G.D. Birla did all he could to create a solid phalanx of Indian businessmen who could speak in a single voice on matters related to economic nationalism. After setting up the Indian Chamber of Commerce in Calcutta in 1926 to counter the British-dominated Bengal Chamber of Commerce and Industry, Birla's finest hour came a year later, in 1927, when he spearheaded the formation of the Federation of Indian Chamber of Commerce and Industry (FICCI) with members from Bombay, Ahmedabad, Kanpur, Delhi and Madras. Some of the members were Purshottamdas Thakurdas (the first president), Walchand Hirachand, Dinshaw Petit, Kasturbhai Lalbhai, Lala Shri Ram, Kamlapat Singhania and M.C.T. Muthiah Chettiar. Even in a racially segregated city like Calcutta, whose corporate world was more British than any other in the country, Indian entrepreneurs had come to stay. And they did, migrating from Burra Bazar in north Calcutta to Rainey Park and then Alipore, building sumptuous houses with huge lawns, much like the sahibs who were now their smarting neighbours.

---

[59] CSAS, Benthall Papers, Box I, 'Monty' Thomas–Edward Benthall, 12 December 1928.
[60] Ibid., Box I, Edward–Paul Benthall, 12 December 1928.

Cotton Mills of Bombay, Ahmedabad and Elsewhere

In sharp contrast to Calcutta, Bombay was a truly cosmopolitan metropolis. From the last quarter of the nineteenth century, Parsi, Gujarati and Marwari entrepreneurs and businessmen were at least as important as their British and European compatriots; and the explicit racial superiority of the British, so obvious in the large offices, restaurants and clubs of Calcutta even up to the late 1960s, was scarcely present in Bombay. Nowhere was this more apparent than in the growth of cotton spinning and weaving mills in Bombay and Ahmedabad.

The manufacturing plunge was taken in July 1854 by Cowasjee Nanabhoy Davar (1815–1873), son of a successful Parsi mercantile trader of Bombay, who floated the Bombay Spinning and Weaving Company in Tardeo with a paid-up capital of Rs 500,000 comprising 100 shares of Rs 5,000 each. The clever businessman that he was, Davar subscribed to the majority of the shares and set about controlling the enterprise like a managing agency. The mill started production in February 1856 under the supervision of British engineers and did well right from its inception.

Seeing Davar's success, others followed.[61] By 1875, there were twenty-two mills in the island of Bombay

---

[61] Davar, incidentally, also started three banks—the Commercial Bank in 1845, the Mercantile Bank in 1853 and the Brokers' Loan Discount and Banking Company in 1861—and installed the first hydraulic press in Bombay in 1853. See Ashok V. Desai,

and, in that year, the mill owners got together to form the Bombay Mill Owners' Association, which was to be the most powerful Indian-dominated textile industry body up to Independence and beyond. Encouraged by the profits of the incumbents, new mills continued to be established in what was to be known as the Girangaon area of Bombay— the central tract of land on the island covering Tardeo, Byculla, Mazgaon, Parel, Lalbaug, Sewri, Prabhadevi and Worli.[62] By 1892, the city had twenty-eight mills with over 445,000 spindles and more than 4,200 looms, supplying both yarn and cloth for the local markets.[63]

Though mostly Indian, Bombay's mill owners came from diverse backgrounds—Parsis, Gujarati Hindus, Baghdadi Jews and even the odd Khoja Ismailis. Some of them, particularly the Parsis and the Baghdadi Jew family of the Sassoons, had made their fortunes in shipping Malwa opium to Canton, and had moved to cotton spinning and weaving from the second half of the nineteenth century. Three Parsi families were most active in Bombay's textile industry: Petit, Wadia and Tata. In 1855, Manekji Petit, a prosperous merchant, founded the Oriental Spinning and Weaving Mill, the first composite mill in the city. It was so successful that his son Dinshaw Manekji Petit (1823–1901) built a second in his father's name in 1860. By the mid-1880s, the younger Petit

---

'The Origins of Parsi Enterprise', *IESHR*, Vol. 5(4), reprinted in Rajat K. Ray (ed.), *Entrepreneurship and Industry in India, 1800– 1947*, Delhi, Oxford University Press, 1992, p. 104.

[62] The word Girangaon literally means the 'village of mills'.

[63] Tripathi and Jumani (2007), p. 60.

controlled six mills and a dyeing house in Mahim, with major interests in yarn and cloth trade. An important civic personality of Bombay in the late nineteenth century, he was knighted in 1887, served as the sheriff of the city, was a member of the Legislative Council and was conferred a baronetcy in 1890.[64]

Sir Dinshaw helped in setting up another mill owner, Nowrosjee Nusserwanji Wadia. Frustrated at the failure of some equipment in one of his mills, he called upon Wadia, a clever young engineer from a wealthy trading and shipbuilding family, to look into the matter. Wadia fixed the problem and also set up a 4,000 horsepower steam engine in one of Sir Dinshaw's mills. By then, young Wadia was hooked on cotton mills. Being rich and having engineering expertise, Wadia soon set up three mills under his control, including the iconic Bombay Dyeing and Manufacturing Mills in 1879, and built ten others.[65]

The biggest Parsi player was doubtless Jamsetji Nusserwanji Tata (1839–1904). His father Nusserwanji, having moved from Navsari to Bombay, had amassed a huge fortune in trading, especially from opium exports to China. The son went many steps further in trade and manufacturing. Being a graduate from Elphinstone

[64] Sir Roper Lethbridge KCIE, *The Golden Book of India: A Genealogical and Biographical Dictionary of the Ruling Princes, Chiefs, Nobles and Other Personages, Titled or Decorated, of the British Empire*, 1893, re-published by Aakar Books, 2005, p. 415.

[65] Tripathi and Jumani (2007), pp. 64–5, and Ashok V. Desai in Rajat K. Ray (1992), p. 104.

College, Bombay, and having spent considerable time in Britain understanding the nuances of textile mills, Jamsetji bought a bankrupt oil mill at Chinchpokli in Bombay in 1869, converting it into a cotton mill. Naming it Alexandra Mill, Tata sold it two years later for a hefty profit.

He then set up the Central India Spinning, Weaving and Manufacturing Company in Nagpur with 14,400 spindles and 450 looms, which was rechristened Empress Mill in 1877 when Queen Victoria became the Empress of India. Though seemingly radical at the time, the choice of Nagpur proved to be brilliant. Berar cotton was close at hand, as was central Indian coal; yarn was sold to many handloom centres close by; and the coarse cloth found local markets without undue competition from either Bombay or Lancashire. Jamsetji introduced ring spindles at Empress Mill long before others did, which dramatically increased spinning productivity. And instead of taking a commission on sales as most managing agencies were wont to do, he took his cut from profits. He acquired two more bankrupt mills, Swadeshi in Bombay and Advance Mill in Ahmedabad, and turned these around quickly enough.

Of the many Hindu mill owners in Bombay, the three most notable of them towards the end of the nineteenth century were Morarjee Goculdas, Damodar Thackersey Mulji and Khatau Makanji. Goculdas set up and took control of the eponymous Morarjee Goculdas Spinning and Weaving Company Limited in 1874 and went on to establish the Sholapur Spinning and Weaving Company. Mulji, a wealthy piece-goods merchant in the city, acquired three mill companies and set up a fourth, the Western India Spinning and Manufacturing Company Limited, in 1880. And Khatau Makanji set up the Khatau Makanji Spinning and Weaving Company in 1874, which was soon to be one of the largest composite units in Bombay.

David Sassoon (1792–1864) escaped with his family from Baghdad to Bombay in 1832, fleeing the ire of a high-ranked noble in Mesopotamia. Initially, his business was dominated by the hugely profitable opium trade to Canton. One of his sons, Elias David (E.D.), after returning to Bombay from a long stint in China, turned his attention to cotton textiles. E.D. started out by purchasing Alexandra Mill in 1874 from Jamestji Tata and renaming it the Sassoon Spinning and Weaving Company; he then went on to promote four more mills, thus becoming a force in the industry.

It wasn't as if there were no British managing agencies engaged in cotton textiles in Bombay. James Finlay & Company managed three mills—Finlay, Gold Mohur and Swan; W.H. Brady & Company also managed three—New Great Eastern, Colaba and the New City of Bombay; Killick Nixon controlled Kohinoor Mills; and Forbes Forbes Campbell & Company managed Simplex Mills. However, unlike in Calcutta, these managing agencies neither dominated the business nor the Bombay Mill Owners Association nor even the social scene.

Now for the industry in Ahmedabad. Here, the pioneer was Ranchhodlal Chhotalal, born in 1812 to a Nagar brahmin family. He, like Dwarkanath Tagore, worked as the senior-most Indian officer of the British government in the Panchmahal area of Gujarat. Accused of taking a bribe in 1853, Ranchhodlal was discharged from service—an event that changed him from a servant of the raj to an industrialist. After years of trying to tie up machinery, technicians and finances, Ranchhodlal finally secured Rs 100,000, of which Rs 25,000 was his own funds, to set up a spinning mill. Dadabhai Naoroji, then in England, was his machinery purchasing agent. He camped in Cambay for nearly three months, supervising the unloading of various machinery, and getting them transported by bullock carts over fifty-two miles to Ahmedabad. Finally, Shahpur Mill was set up in 1861. For his services, Ranchhodlal put in place a managing agency which, in addition to running the mill, would receive 2.5 per cent from the sale of yarn. The mill was profitable, which encouraged him to build another. Ranchhodlal died in 1898, the richest man in Ahmedabad, a member of the Bombay Legislative Council, office-bearer of the Indian National Congress, donor to various charities and a Companion of the Indian Empire.[66]

Ranchhodlal's success spawned others'. His friend Becherdas Ambaidas, who had a commission to supply grain to the army of the East India Company, expanded first to cotton trading and then set up the second mill in Ahmedabad in 1867. By 1892, the city had eleven mills with over 289,000 spindles and almost 4,500 looms. The

[66] Howard Spodek, 'The "Manchesterisation" of Ahmedabad', *The Economic Weekly*, 13 March 1965, pp. 483–84.

next thirteen years saw even more rapid growth. In 1905, Ahmedabad had thirty-two mills employing around 21,500 workers, with more than 577,000 spindles and over 7,200 looms. The mills were all run and controlled by Gujarati managing agencies. The city's textile industry now accounted for 15 per cent of the country's capacity.[67]

By 1902–03 the cotton textile industry, controlled almost wholly by Indians, located mostly in the Bombay Presidency and highly concentrated in Bombay and Ahmedabad, accounted for over 4.7 million spindles and 39,000 looms. The largest factory-based industry in India, it employed an average of 181,000 workers per day to produce 1.44 million bales of saleable yarn (each of 400 lbs) and 406 million yards of woven cloth. In terms of net value added, it accounted for Rs 184 million at constant 1938–39 prices, or 38 per cent of net output produced by all of modern manufacturing in the country, and over 8 per cent of the entire secondary sector output. For all its importance, especially in foreign trade, jute was a poor second—less than one-third the size of the cotton mills industry, with a net value added of Rs 60 million.[68]

The cotton mills grew at a rapid pace right up to the end of the 1920s, as Chart C shows. The chart also demonstrates a fundamental change that was occurring in the industry—a strong shift away from saleable yarn and in favour of woven cloth. Between 1900–01 and 1929–30, the production of yarn for sale grew at a compound annual

[67] *Ibid.*, pp. 485–86.
[68] Computed from Sivasubramonian (2000), Tables 4.3, 4.8, 4.10 and 4.44.

trend rate of 1.1 per cent; in contrast, production of woven textiles expanded at 6.2 per cent per year. By the end of the period, the role of Manchester as the prime supplier of cloth to India was being seriously challenged by the composite mills of the Bombay Presidency and elsewhere, causing considerable heartburn in England.

Chart C: Mill output of saleable yarn and cloth

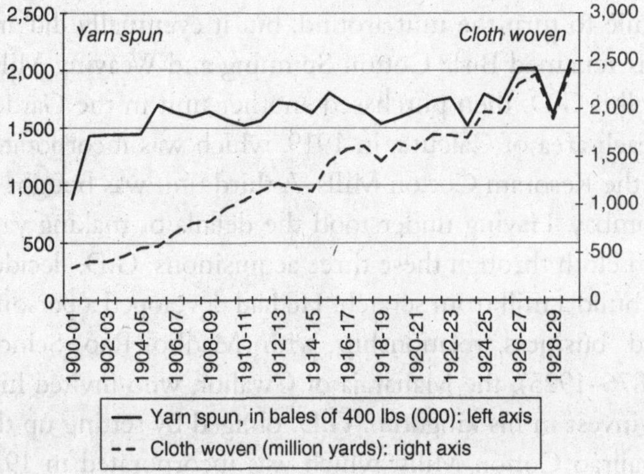

Source: Sivasubramonian (2000), Table 4.3

Though Bombay and Ahmedabad led the industry, cotton mills were coming up rapidly in various parts of India. Curzon's partitioning of Bengal in 1905 started a swadeshi movement in Dacca and Calcutta whose economic expression was to be found in the setting up of factories to liberate the land from British imports. In 1908, Mohini Mohan Chakravarty, a relatively well-to-do brahmin, raised capital for setting up Mohini Mills, at Kushtia in the district of Nadia, which began production some years later. In the inter-war years, the enterprise opened a second unit at Belghoria in the north-eastern outskirts of Calcutta. Others followed: Bengal Luxmi Cotton Mills at Serampore under the Bengal Textile Agency, Dhakeshwari Cotton Mills at Naraingunj near Dacca and Basanti Cotton Mills at Panihati.[69]

Sir Sarupchand Hukumchand set up three cotton mills in his home town Indore. In 1916, G.D. Birla took over the Gilhari, a sick cotton mill in Delhi; it took a long while to turn the unit around, but it eventually did and was renamed Birla Cotton Spinning and Weaving Mills, Delhi. G.D. then purchased another unit in the Garden Reach area of Calcutta in 1919, which was incorporated as the Kesoram Cotton Mills. A third unit was bought in Bombay. Having understood the details of making yarn and cloth through these three acquisitions, G.D. decided to build a mill from scratch. He had developed a personal and business relationship with Madho Rao Scindia (1876–1925), the Maharaja of Gwalior, who invited him to invest in his kingdom. G.D. obliged by setting up the Jiyajirao Cotton Mills, which was incorporated in 1921 and started production a couple of years later.

During this period, Lala Shri Ram (1884–1963) exemplified the case of a person who grew from the ranks to become an entrepreneur. It is a story in itself. His father Madan Mohan Lall was a relatively modest bania who worked in Delhi as a salaried secretary of the Delhi Cloth and General Mills (DCM). Shri Ram tried his hand at two early ventures, both of which failed miserably. Instead of

[69] *Investor's India Year Book (IIYB), 1945–47*, section on cotton.

depending on his family for his sustenance, he took up a clerical job with a firm of contractors that made its money by supplying tents for the coronation Durbar of 1911. He apparently so impressed Boota Singh the proprietor that Singh, on finding out that Shri Ram was Madan Mohan's son, prevailed upon the father to allow the lad to be trained at DCM.

The company was performing abjectly at the time. A superb manager and workaholic, Shri Ram soon made a name for himself in the company and, by the eve of World War I, had become the de facto secretary of DCM. The war was the turning point. Shri Ram decided to weave tents to supply the army. Since all major army contracts were supplied through middlemen, Shri Ram created a three-way partnership involving DCM, Diwan Chand, who was such a middleman, and his father. According to this arrangement—a clever variation of the managing agency—DCM would produce tents, Shri Ram in his own capacity would procure additional items as needed by the army, and Diwan Chand would be the funnel for supplying these items to the army. The profits from these three streams were pooled and shared in the ratio of 50 per cent to DCM, 30 per cent to Diwan Chand and 20 per cent to Madan Mohan. DCM's profits soared, as did the family's. With his money, Lala Shri Ram increased his stake in DCM to 16 per cent, which was enough to give him effective control over the company.[70]

[70] From en.wikipedia.org/wiki/Lala_Shri_Ram; and Tripathi and Jumani (2007), p. 101.

Lala Shri Ram didn't stop there. A fire in the DCM factory in 1920 provided an opportunity to begin full-fledged reconstruction of the mill. He replaced the old machinery with new, then set up a bleaching plant and a dye house that went on-stream in 1924. A year later he set up another unit next to the original mill. DCM had come of age, thanks to the young Lala Shri Ram.

Kanpur, then a large cantonment town in the United Provinces, also saw the growth of industry during this period. Towards the end of the nineteenth century, Sir John Burney Allen established a group of companies including Cawnpore Textiles, Cawnpore Woollen Mills (which produced the once famous Lal-imli brand), Elgin Mills, Flex Shoes Company and North Tannery, all under the British India Corporation headquartered in the city.

The twentieth century saw an upsurge of Indian entrepreneurship. By the second half of the 1920s, Lala Kamlapat Singhania started several enterprises such as J.K. Cotton Mills, J.K. Jute and J.K. Iron under the banner of Juggilal Kamlapat. During the same period, Jwala Prasad Srivastava (1889–1954), a UP *kayastha*, having working as an industrial chemist for the provincial government, chose to become an industrialist. He established the New Victoria Mills in Kanpur, several dyeing works, the Raza Textile Mills in the princely state of Rampur, and two other mills in Gwalior and Bhopal, all of which were organized under the managing agency of J.P. Srivastava & Sons. Jwala Prasad, a perfect kayastha brown sahib of his times, served the provincial and imperial government in various capacities, and soon became Sir J.P. Srivastava, Knight Commander of the Star of India.[71]

The Jaipurias bought the Swadeshi Cotton Mills from the Horsman family, which was then managed by Bagla, Jaipuria & Company.

What kind of share ownership did managing agencies have across the cotton textile industry? Table 2 provides some data. As in jute, most of the mill companies were controlled by entities with low share ownership: in sixteen of the twenty-three listed companies in this sample, managing agencies owned less than 20 per cent of the voting stock; and in seven, less than 10 per cent. It was in only seven out of the twenty-three that the managing agency's ownership exceed 30 per cent, and in just three a clear 50 per cent-plus majority.

Table 2: Shareholding of Managing Agencies in Cotton Textile, c.1930

Mill Company	Managing Agent	Equity Shareholding of the Managing Agent
Colaba Land & Mill	W.H. Brady & Co.	0.3%
Bengal Nagpur Cotton Mills	Shaw Wallace & Co.	4.8%
Vishnu Cotton Mills	The Bombay Co.	6.8%
Central India	Tata Sons	8.0%
Crescent Mills	Currimbhai Ebrahim & Sons	8.6%
Bowreah Cotton Mills	Kettlewell, Bullen & Co.	8.9%

---

[71] From en.wikipedia.org/wiki/Jwala_Prasad_Srivastava.

Mill Company	Managing Agent	Equity Shareholding of the Managing Agent
Bombay Dyeing & Manufacturing	Nowrosjee Wadia & Sons	9.8%
Swadeshi Mills	Tata Sons	10.2%
Ahmedabad Advance Mills	Tata Sons	10.4%
Fazulbhoi Mills	Currimbhai Ebrahim & Sons	11.3%
Ebrahim Pabaney Mills	Currimbhai Ebrahim & Sons	14.0%
Hindustan Spinning & Weaving Mills	Thackersay, Moolji & Co.	14.7%
Bradbury Mills	Currimbhai Ebrahim & Sons	15.6%
Tata Mills	Tata Sons	16.8%
Edward Sassoon Mills	E.D. Sassoon & Co.	17.1%
Dunbar Mills	Kettlewell, Bullen & Co.	19.3%
Gokak Mills	Forbes Forbes, Campbell & Co.	32.3%
Coorla Spinning & Weaving	Cowasjee Jehangir & Co.	34.2%
Century Spinning & Manufacturing	C.N. Wadia & Sons	43.5%
Currimbhai Mills	Currimbhai Ebrahim & Sons	47.8%
Dawn Mills	David Sassoon & Co.	54.1%
Framji Petit Mills	D.M. Petit & Sons	57.4%
David Mills	E.D. Sassoon & Co.	74.0%
Median Share Ownership		**14.7%**

Source: Lokanathan (1935), pp. 42–43.

Iron and Steel

From the early 1880s, it had been Jamsetji Tata's vision to make steel in India. Nearly two decades later, he acquired prospecting rights in the district of Chanda in the Bombay Presidency, only to find that the iron ore was unsuitable for smelting. A more promising eastern site was found near Durg, east of Raipur, in what is now the district of Chhattisgarh. It proved to have large reserves of exactly the right kind of ore. That set the stage for starting an iron and steel mill at a site near the village of Sakchi in Bihar. Jamsetji passed away in 1904, and the task of producing steel fell upon his eldest son Sir Dorabji Tata (1859–1932).

Foreign equity was very hard to come by; so too the requisite support from bankers for a project of this size. Dorabji tried his best to sell the idea in the City of London but returned empty-handed. That was when something happened—a clear demonstration of the change in attitude among the moneyed in India.

Dorabji issued a public appeal to the citizens of India. It worked. Shares of the Tata Iron and Steel Company Limited (TISCO), under the managing agency of Tata Sons, offered to the public on 26 August 1907 were oversubscribed in just three weeks. For the first time in the financial history of the country, Indian citizens joined hands to finance an enterprise of this size: 89 per cent of the paid-up capital was bought by thousands of Indian shareholders, big and small, with the remaining 11 per cent being contributed by the Tata family. With a capacity of 100,000 ingots, the blast furnaces started operations in late 1911. TISCO rolled out its first steel ingot in February 1912.

The story of TISCO is remarkable not only on account of the huge support that it got from Indian shareholders but also for the help that it often received from the raj. For a start, the government, in 1910, contributed by connecting a Bengal Nagpur Railway feeder line between the plant and the iron ore mines. On numerous occasions thereafter, the raj—from the Viceroy to other civil servants—went out of their way to help the enterprise. As Amiya Bagchi puts it, 'The representatives of both the British government and the nationalists used superlatives in describing the achievements of TISCO . . . It grew up without tariff protection in its infancy, weathered the crisis of the years 1923–34 under the umbrella of protection and then dispensed with protection altogether.'[72] To be sure, TISCO enjoyed significant cost advantages vis-à-vis imported steel. In the absence of competition from Europe and the US, it ramped up to full capacity utilization during World War I to supply rails, shells, wheels and even ferromanganese to the Government of India.[73] While this did not translate into a substantial rise in profits because of price-controlled rates, the act of supplying as much as 90 per cent of its output to the government according to strict British technical specifications met with widespread

[72] Bagchi (1972), p. 291.
[73] During the war, TISCO's blast furnaces were often producing 250 tons of pig iron per day versus a rated capacity of 175 tons. *Ibid.*, p. 305.

official approval. That was to come very useful to the company shortly after the war.

The war boom made TISCO think of expanding its steel-making capacity from 150,000 tons to 250,000, which came to be known as the company's Greater Extensions. Though the Government of India and the Railway Board gave TISCO the green light, most of the equipment could not reach the country till Armistice Day in November 1918. In a year or two, TISCO was in deep trouble—focusing on a huge expansion in pig iron and steel-making capacity at a time when European and American steel came back to India. The competition was intense, with TISCO at the receiving end.

In 1923, TISCO asked the Indian Tariff Board (ITB) for tariff protection of 33.33 per cent on all imported steel. The ITB acquiesced, but at a lower rate which, while helpful, did not suffice to counter imports of continental steel at depreciated exchange rates. TISCO asked for additional protection in 1924, which it got for a period of three years that was extended for another three. This period, often called one of 'discriminating tariff protection' showed up three things. First, the goodwill that TISCO and the House of Tata enjoyed with the colonial government. Second, the very clever economics of the ITB; the protective tariffs being regularly brought down in line with reductions in the domestic cost of production showed ITB's ability to discriminate with the changing times. Third, the use of discriminating tariff protection as a lever to induce TISCO to continuously raise productivity while reducing fixed as well as operating costs, which the company did very successfully.[74] Through this process, TISCO expanded, stabilized and then became the most cost-efficient producer of steel in India.

TISCO was not the only steel producer in India. In 1918, a managing agency called Burn & Company (later by Martin Burn), controlled in large measure by Sir Rajendra Nath Mookerjee (1854–1936), a hugely successful engineer, builder and contractor in eastern India, floated the Indian Iron and Steel Company Limited (IISCO) to manufacture pig iron and steel at Kulti, near Asansol in Bengal. Steel was kept in abeyance through the early years, with IISCO focusing on producing saleable pig iron. These two enterprises were later followed by a smaller unit called the Mysore Iron and Steel Works with its plant at Bhadravati. Soon enough, the three got into an informal cartel to carve up markets and control prices.

Though much was written about the cartel by the contemporary press, it is doubtful whether the combine actually succeeded in maintaining prices, especially with enormous differences in pig iron demand in the eastern, western, southern and northern regions of India. And the advent of the Great Depression put paid to all cartels. Be

[74] Bagchi correctly points out that 'the credit for a large part of the fall in cost of production [of steel] must be given to successive Tariff Boards appointed by the Government of India: TISCO was compelled to reduce costs because at every stage the tariffs or bounties proposed were just enough to cover the prime costs of production plus a given percentage of the replacement value of capital and the working capital the Tariff Board considered necessary.' *Ibid.*, p. 319.

that as it may, by the end of 1929, the Indian iron and steel industry had arrived on the scene—organized largely by Indian managing agencies, run by Indian promoters and supported by Indian shareholders, a situation that was beyond the pale of imagination a few decades earlier.

PART II: DEPRESSION, WAR AND INDEPENDENCE, 1930–47

Jute Mills

The depression hit the jute industry as it was enjoying the fruits of a long boom. The IJMA had increased permissible working hours from fifty-four to sixty per week; loomage had increased substantially, and two new mills had been commissioned, both under Indian ownership and control. Then suddenly, the earth vanished under their feet. The mills, long used to complacently operating in a world of increasing demand and high profits, found themselves with blank order books and sheds full of raw jute uncovered by gunny sales. In 1930 alone, the volume of gunny bag exports dropped by 17 per cent and cloth by 23 per cent, with prices falling by 19 per cent and 32 per cent, respectively.[75] It was just the beginning of a horrendous period that ended with the onset of World War II.

Unlike many industries in India and elsewhere in the world, the Depression, for jute, did not come to an end by

[75] Goswami (1991), p. 127. As earlier, this section on jute is based on Goswami (1982, 1985, 1989 and 1991).

1934 but continued right up to 1939. It had much to do with the very nature of the product. However profitable it might have been in good years, gunny bags and cloth were merely cheap material for packing other primary products. With the sharply falling global prices of primary goods, it was no surprise that gunny prices fell further and for longer. Through the depression, prices of gunny bag and cloth were half of their average price during 1925–29.

The IJMA behaved predictably. It first reduced working hours at its member mills from sixty to fifty-four per week. That did precious little, so it instructed all mills to down shutters for one week each month. Even that did not help. Working hours were further reduced to forty per week, and members were ordered to seal 15 per cent of their looms. In a trice, all hell broke loose.

During 1928–29, five large jute mills had been commissioned near Calcutta, four under Indian managing agencies and were members of the IJMA; and one, Agarpara, under B.N. Elias & Company, set up by a Baghdadi Jew, which was not with IJMA. When the IJMA asked Agarpara to join, the mill requested special dispensation to add seventy-five looms that it was about to install and to operate some extra hours over the work time limit. The Association refused. Agarpara immediately installed the extra looms and began to work 108 hours per week. Other mills followed suit, and by 1931 the four new mills quit the IJMA and increased their working hours to 108 per week. It was a ridiculously asymmetric situation, where the cartel members were working only forty hours per week, with 15 per cent of their looms sealed and a forced closure of seven days per month, while the interlopers were making merry. In 1931–32, the non-IJMA mills accounted for less than 3 per cent of the industry's output, but by 1934–35, their share rose significantly, crossing 10 per cent thanks to the IJMA's masochism.

The IJMA had got its economics all wrong. It is impossible to implement tough production quotas in an acute depression when members have very different fixed and variable costs. It is even more impractical when the product in question is a commoditized packing material. Besides, this was being attempted at a time when the importing world was rapidly moving to bulk-handling. Only arrogant and ill-schooled expatriates in a cocooned corporate enclave called Calcutta could believe that such tactics would work. These did not, and profits slumped. Between 1925 and 1929, the forty jute mill companies listed in the *Investor's India Year Book* had earned an average annual net profit of almost 40 per cent of their paid-up capital. By 1930, this figure had dipped below 21 per cent. A year later, in 1931, it crashed to 4.8 per cent, marginally improving to 5.7 per cent in 1932. By then, things had become so bad that most mills stopped providing for depreciation to create unreal profits and declare dividends that were not earned at all.

Why did the British managing agencies declare dividends during a time of losses? The answer lies in one word: fear. By that time it was clear that Indians, especially Marwaris, were seriously getting into the industry—either by direct entry or through steady purchase of jute mill

company shares whose prices had slumped to less than 50
per cent of their peak values in 1928. Steeply south-bound
shares were being sold by pessimists who saw no respite to
the downturn, and were bought by Marwaris. Even more
worrisome was that many large Marwari banias who had
lent working capital to many of the managing agencies in
the 1920s started calling for more cover, which threatened
to further dilute British control. In these desperate times,
the British managing agencies believed that declaring large
dividends would help shore up share prices. Thus, in the
five years between 1930 and 1934, British-managed jute
mill companies spent over Rs 30 million from their reserve
funds to declare dividends that bore no relationship with
the loss-making reality. When a second slump occurred
in 1937–38, whatever was left in reserves was paid out
in bloated dividends. The strategy failed miserably; share
prices did not pick up until the beginning of World War II,
and the Marwaris continued to increase their shareholding
in these companies throughout the period.

In 1932, the IJMA, in its desperation to hammer out an
agreement to accommodate the five 'truant' mills offered
to allow them to work fifty-four hours a week with all
their looms while the loyal members of the Association
were to continue to cap their working hours at forty per
week and keep 15 per cent of their looms sealed. The
agreement was doomed to fail for, at that point, there
were nineteen other mills outside the IJMA with over
6,000 looms working up to 108 hours per week. To the
enraged Scots of the industry, their cosy business and
venerable Association seemed to have degenerated into

a disgraceful, chaotic bazaar, with 'pedlars, packmen and *bikriwallah*s each fighting for his own hand'.[76]

The IJMA's situation in the 1930s—dramatically falling world demand, cartel failure and the steady entry of native Indians in what just a decade or so ago was a 'whites-only' industry—was brilliantly illustrated by a cartoon in a magazine called *Capital*. The interloping Indian mills were apparently selling poorer quality of burlap at lower prices in the US. This prompts an angry Uncle Sam with a big stick to confront a trembling, kilted Scot.

Uncle Sam:	(*Holding an offending piece of burlap*) Who did this?
Scot:	(*Trembling*). Please, Sir! It was not I. It was my boss. (*Points to a dhoti-clad, betel-chewing Marwari with a pugree and a paunch*)
Uncle Sam:	(Incredulously) Is *that* your boss?
Scot:	Yes, Sir. I can't do any business without his blessings.
Uncle Sam:	(*Whipping the Scot on his kilted posterior*) Serves you right, you stupid fool, for having such a boss![77]

This crazy situation could not have lasted. In 1936, Birla and Hukumchand forced the pace by handing in their conditional resignation from the IJMA. They argued that

[76] IJMA, Report of the Committee 1930 (Calcutta, 1931), speech of the President, A. Sime, p. 8.
[77] *Capital*, 16 November 1933, p. 797.

the only way to deal with the outsiders was to allow all
member mills to work unrestricted hours to bring the
interlopers to heel. Soon enough, led by the Bird-Heilgers
group and supported by Andrew Yule & Company, others
came around to this point of view, accommodation having
come to naught. In March 1937 all output and capacity
restrictions were withdrawn and a ruthless free-for-all
started in the industry. Output shot up by 39 per cent
above the 1935–36 level; prices fell by 19 per cent; profits
crashed; and by 1938, all but seven of the forty listed jute
mill companies had reported losses. Thereafter, the IJMA
used its influence on Huseyn Shaheed Suhrawardy—
the minister of commerce and labour under the new
provincial government led by Fazlul Huq—who was
beholden to the mills through a long line of graft. He
piloted the Bengal Jute Ordinance in September 1938 to
statutorily restrict work hours. Battle scarred, bereft of
profits and forced by law, all mills began to toe the line.
How long they would have complied with the law in what
was still an era of excess supply remains an unanswered
question. That was not to be tested because, a year later,
Adolf Hitler's troops crossed into Poland and the demand
for sandbags started yet again.

Like World War I, World War II too was a boon for the
industry. In the first six months of the war, the jute mills
supplied 923 million bags and 45 million yards of cloth
on war orders alone. By April 1945, military demand
had fetched the industry revenue worth Rs 759 million.
Even more money was made in civilian exports to the
US and elsewhere. The Calcutta price of burlap rose by

over 125 per cent between 1935–38 and 1939–45; and that
of gunny bags by 127 per cent. Again back to big money
making, average net profits as a share of paid-up capital
for the listed jute mill companies, as documented in the
Investor's India Year Book, rose; it was 39 per cent in 1940;
46 per cent in 1941; 52 per cent in 1942; 41 per cent in
1943; 45 per cent in 1944; and 44 per cent in 1945. Bulk
of the profits was used to declare huge dividends—mostly
because the expatriates were unsure of their fate in a soon-
to-be independent India and preferred to repatriate as
much as they could. Two years after the end of World War
II, India gained independence, putting the jute mills in a
quandary. After Partition, India had all the mills, mostly
around Calcutta, while over three-quarters of the jute
growing area went to East Pakistan. That created its own
supply side problems, which took over a decade-and-a-
half to sort out, when the fields of lower Assam, West
Bengal and parts of Andhra Pradesh picked up the slack.

The most fascinating aspect of the story of the jute
industry in the period following World War I is the
growth of Indian, especially Marwari, entrepreneurship
and control in a sector that was earlier run exclusively by
British managing agencies. In 1911, more than 97 per cent
of the board positions in listed jute mill companies were
held by British men.[78] By December 1930, 56 per cent
of the expatriate mill companies had Marwari directors,
and 59 per cent of all listed jute mills had at least one

[78] The *Census of India 1911*, Vol. I (1), p. 446; and the *Investor's
India Year Book 1919*.

Marwari on the board. Table 3 contains the data, clearly demonstrating how the Indians systematically got into this industry. It should be noted that the table understates Marwari control, for it ignores several unlisted mill companies that came into being during 1928–1939, and were run by Indians, mostly Marwaris. If all units were to be taken into account, then by 1945, Indians exclusively owned and controlled twenty-five of the country's eighty-five jute mill companies, or 29 per cent of the enterprises.

Table 3: Changes in directorial positions in listed jute mill companies

	1930	1942	1945	1948	1951	1957
Indian companies (% of total)	5%	20%	24%	24%	25%	29%
Expatriate companies with Marwari directors (% of such companies)	56%	62%	82%	89%	89%	86%
Expatriate companies under de facto Marwari control*	2%	5%	15%	15%	17%	17%
Companies with Marwari directors (% of total)	59%	63%	80%	85%	86%	89%

Source: Investor's India Year Book, successive years, from Goswami (1991), Table 7.3, p. 180.

Note: *An expatriate company in which the majority on the board were Marwaris. Such entities were effectively controlled by the Marwaris though the old names and registered office addresses were maintained.

Table 3 shows something else that is equally important for our understanding of the history of this industry. Much of the change in ownership and control occurred between 1930 and 1945 and not immediately, nor even a decade, after Independence. As the table shows, changes between 1945 and 1957 were far more modest compared with those of 1930–45. The financially stronger and better organized expatriate managing agencies such as Bird-Heilgers, Andrew Yule, Macneill & Barry, Jardine and Thomas Duff stayed on after 1947 and fared reasonably well until the early 1960s when they were finally taken over by the Marwaris. Those that packed up shortly after Independence did not do so because of the demise of the raj, but on account of their financial strains and operational inefficiencies that had begun with the Depression and continued thereafter. Many of them were actually purchased by their old banias: Kettlewell Bullen by Bangur; Anderson Wright by Kedia; Begg Dunlop by Bajoria; Duncan by Keshav Prasad Goenka; and McLeod by Radha Kissen Kanoria.

More than any other tale, the story of the post-World War I jute industry belongs to the Marwaris. It tells of how they built their finances through their deep and wide connections in the raw jute and gunny trade, their speculation and fatka to move into the world of manufacturing in an industry where there were no technical barriers to entry; of how, with the exception of G.D. Birla, they steadily increased their control over the industry while remaining seemingly subservient to the whites; and of how decisively they transformed from players in the world of trade into entrepreneurs who sat in the board rooms of corporations. All this happened during the colonial era, in a city where the whites ruled supreme. In the history of nationalist industrialization, the pride of place is reserved for cotton textiles and steel, and hardly ever jute. The facts suggest otherwise. Other than Birla, the Marwaris in jute were not hardcore nationalists. But they did a great deal to raise the native colours in an export-driven industry where they were least expected to.

To my mind, the greatest and most perceptive tribute to the Marwaris came from a British man, as early as in 1906, well before they had entered the business of jute manufacturing in Calcutta. In a letter to H.N. Gladstone, the London-based managing partner of Gillanders Arbuthnot, a Calcutta partner called William Wickham wrote, 'The man to whom business is all in all, food and drink, is the Marwari, not the ordinary European merchant.'[79]

Cotton Mills

Unlike the jute business, the cotton textile industry was barely touched by the Depression. As Chart D shows, from the end of World War I till Independence, while net value added from the jute industry did not grow at all, the cotton textile industry kept growing at an impressive exponential trend rate of 3.9 per cent per year. The reason for this difference is not hard to find. Jute, a bargain-basement material exported to pack primary products,

[79] Misra (1999), p. 17.

faced the full brunt of the collapse in global trade. In contrast, cotton yarn and cloth, necessities manufactured exclusively for the Indian markets, were by and large immune to the slump. This is evident from the data in Table 4.

Chart D: Net value added, cotton and jute industries

Rs million at 1938–39 prices

Trend growth rate: 3.9% per year

Trend growth rate: 0% per year

— Net value added, cotton
- - - Net value added, jute

Source: *Sivasubramonian (2000), Chapter 4*

As the table shows, the country's textile industry continued to expand during the time when jute was in the doldrums. Over the period shown in the table, the average number of spindles as well as looms grew by 34 per cent. Productivity growth was even more impressive: both saleable yarn and cloth output increased well in excess of 90 per cent. And the industry expanded fast enough for the average workforce to rise by 35 per cent. It was a remarkable achievement of Indian enterprise.

Table 4: Growth of the cotton mill industry 1927–28 to 1946–47

Average for	Spindles (000)	Looms (000)	Saleable yarn, bales of 400 lbs. (000)	Cloth woven (million yards)	Persons employed (000)
1927/28–1929/30	7,147	139	1,909	2,223	364
1930/31–1932/33	8,206	161	2,375	2,907	399
1933/34 –1935/36	8,263	170	2,484	3,304	406
1936/37–1938/39	8,776	181	2,931	3,975	432
1939/40–1941/42	8,699	183	3,467	4,259	457
1942/43–1944/45	9,454	189	4,054	4,569	506
1945/46–1946/47	9,566	186	3,691	4,283	492

Source: Sivasubramonian (2000), Table 4.3.

Other than being a key businessman associated with the freedom movement, Kasturbhai Lalbhai (1894–1980) played a significant role in the growth of the Ahmedabad industry. Belonging to a wealthy yet parsimonious Jain family, his father's early death propelled Kasturbhai into cotton textiles, the family business. Soon sibling rivalries led to the splitting of all personal and business assets and, by 1920, Kasturbhai started with a clean slate.

At the time the largest mill in the city was the Ahmedabad Manufacturing and Calico Printing Company, known as the Calico Mill under the control of Ambalal Sarabhai. Kasturbhai started a new mill in the early 1920s, and then went on to acquire or promote five more mills between 1924 and 1935. He set up Aruna and Nutan; purchased Ahmedabad New Cotton, which was on the brink of bankruptcy; bought out Saraspur, a mill founded by his father, in a liquidation sale; and then engaged in his greatest venture—the setting up of Arvind Mills. Promoted in 1931 with a share capital of over Rs 2.5 million, Arvind became the most modern mill in Ahmedabad and, along with Sarabhai's Calico, produced fine and superfine cloth. By 1938, Kasturbhai was the city's leading industrialist, with seven mills that accounted for 12 per cent of the country's spindles and almost a quarter of its weaving capacity. In terms of net assets, Kasturbhai's was also the thirteenth largest Indian business house of the time, and the fifth largest in textiles.[80]

The inter-war years saw heightened global competition from Japanese fabrics. The worst hit were the Lancashire mills, which faced 'triple jeopardy': of competing with Japan's superior productivity, the low labour costs of Indian mills; and a falling yen. In response, the British government called a trade conference in Ottawa in 1932. The Ottawa Pact of August 1932 hiked import duties on non-British textiles entering India from 31.25 per cent to 50 per cent, while pegging them at 25 per cent, inclusive of surcharge, for Lancashire cloth. It did not work. The Japanese mills continued to take advantage of a steadily depreciating yen to grow exports to India, in response to which the duty on non-British import was increased further to 75 per cent. Even so, Lancashire could not increase its hold on the Indian market.

[80] From en.wikipedia.org/wiki/Kasturbhai_Lalbhai; and Piramal (1998).

Desperate now, Britain sent a Textile Mission to India in 1933 under Sir William Clare-Lees to hammer out a trade agreement with the Indian mill owners. One group of Indian mills, led by nationalist businessmen such as Kasturbhai Lalbhai and G.D. Birla, representing FICCI, opposed any differential concessions in favour of Lancashire; while another, the Bombay Mill Owners Association, led by its long-time president Homi Mody of the Tata Group, was willing to accommodate. Huge disagreements broke out between Lalbhai and Mody, and soon enough Lalbhai left the table, never to return. Mody concluded the negotiation. The Lees-Mody Pact of 1933 gave Lancashire several concessions for British exports of cotton, rayon and artificial silk fabrics to India in exchange for some vague promises, such as that of England buying more raw cotton from the subcontinent. The nationalist press tore the pact apart. Mody was called a lackey of Lancashire, and even more outrage followed when he was knighted shortly afterwards in 1935. In effect, however, the Lees-Mody pact did little to help Lancashire's trade with India, with the import of British textiles falling from an average of 1,400 million yards per annum during the five years preceding the Depression to 552 million yards in 1934–35, and then to 206 million yards in 1938–39.[81] The nation's demand was being increasingly met by its own mills.

By the time of Independence, the industry exhibited certain clear characteristics. First, other than some mills in

[81] Bagchi (1972), Table 7.5, p. 238.

Kanpur, Bombay, Bengal and Madras, it was significantly dominated by Indian entrepreneurs. For all intents and purposes, this industry, accounting for 22 per cent of net added value in organized manufacturing, and for over 11 per cent of secondary sector output in 1946–47, was Indian-owned and controlled. Second, over the years, especially after World War I, the mills of Ahmedabad and Bombay steadily increased their weaving, bleaching and dyeing capacities to become composite mills in the true sense of the term. Almost all of them also sold yarn, and often in significant quantities; but the mills were now predominantly manufacturers of grey or finished cloth. So too were most of the mills in Delhi, Kanpur, the United Provinces, Punjab, Central Provinces and Bengal.[82] Third, thanks to the growth of this Indian-dominated enterprise, the country's dependence on imports fell quite drastically. In 1900–01, 2 billion yards of cloth was imported, which was to exceed 3 billion yards before the outbreak of World War I. By the beginning of the Depression this had dropped to less than 900 million yards; and fell further to under 600 million on the eve of World War II. In effect, India had become more or less self-sufficient in draping its people.[83]

[82] The significant exception was Coimbatore, where mills came into being from the 1920s thanks to the entrepreneurial drive of the Kama Naidus. Given their experience in growing cotton, ginning, baling and trading, it was a relatively small step to set up spinning mills to produce coarse lower count yarn for the numerous handloom weaving centres that dotted the Madras Presidency, Kerala and Mysore.

[83] Bagchi (1972), p. 238.

Construction, Shipping, Sugar and Cement

There can be no story about India's corporate growth from the late 1920s without Walchand Hirachand Doshi (1882–1953), certainly the feistiest and perhaps the most visionary among the country's entrepreneurs, the businessman with probably the greatest risk-taking *chutzpah* of them all. The son of Hirachand Doshi, a cotton trader, moneylender and the local agent of Sholapur Mill that was under the managing agency of Morarjee Goculdas, Walchand completed his matriculation and was admitted to St Xavier's College, Bombay, for a BA degree, but dropped out after a couple of years. Hirachand tried to get his already headstrong son into the world of trade. But that was not for the young man, who was now married for the second time (his first wife had passed away). Walchand, at twenty-one, needed to do new things.

An opportunity came his way when Laxmanrao Balwant Phatak, an ex-railway employee, approached him in 1903 for earnest money to bid for a Rs 80,000 tender for laying a seven-mile narrow gauge railway track. Despite his father's objections, Walchand loaned the money, personally supervised all aspects of the construction, and decided this was his kind of business. Over the next fourteen years, Walchand and Phatak successfully engaged in several major construction projects: rail tracks, first from Bori Bunder to Currey Road in Bombay, and then to Thana and Kalyan, and then the technically difficult harbour branch line; and, during World War I, barracks and hospitals for the army across the Bombay Presidency.

But being a successful contractor was not enough. Walchand wanted to do bigger things.[84]

In January 1919, on hearing that *SS Loyalty*, a steamship owned by the Scindias of Gwalior, was up for sale, he went to inspect the craft. Enamoured by the ship and excited by the idea of starting global shipping out of India, Walchand roped in three partners—Narottam Morarjee, Lallubhai Samaldas and Kilachand Devchand—to purchase the ship and form the Scindia Steam Navigation Company. The company's share flotation was a huge success and it raised Rs 18.7 million, the second largest amount of paid-up capital after Tata Steel's. The managing agency was Narottam Morarjee & Company, in which Walchand's share was 25 per cent. It was a hellishly difficult business that Walchand was getting into.

Several local coastal shipping companies had started operations only to close down. The reason was always one company: the powerful British India Steam Navigation Company. Walchand's foe was James Mackay, the Earl of Inchcape, who was a gutsy, ruthless, 'no-quarters-given' entrepreneur running Mackinnon Mackenzie & Company as well as the much larger Inchcape group, and who had the added advantage of being a Scot operating in colonial India. He considered Walchand's enterprise to be nothing more than 'shameless bluster' and 'downright piracy', and was determined to make this upstart Indian

---

[84] Much of Walchand Hirachand here, both the man and his business, is based on the excellent work by Gita Piramal. See Piramal (1998), section on Walchand Hirachand.

pay the price. It was no false threat. By the time Scindia had mustered a fleet of two passenger ships and six cargo steamers, British India began ruthless rate wars on every route that Scindia plied. Walchand attempted to mobilize nationalist public opinion, mainly through newspapers. In 1923, Inchcape attempted a buyout, but Walchand and Narottam Morarjee prevailed upon the shareholders to refuse. There was a furious verbal battle between Inchcape and Walchand when they met in Delhi in March 1923. Eventually, a temporary truce was offered by Inchcape, which allowed Scindia the right to carry cargo along the coasts of India, Ceylon and Burma.

Had Walchand remained only in shipping, he would have been financially ruined. It was a very competitive and difficult business in the best of times. Luckily for him, construction activity picked up in Bombay, thanks to the Backbay Reclamation Scheme. Sir Dorabji Tata formed Tata Construction to bid for the scheme and invited Walchand as a co-promoter. The company did not get the Rs 300 million contract as the government farmed most of it out to its own public works department, but it succeeded in first winning the Tansa-to-Bombay water pipeline project and then the Bhor Ghat tunnel works from Khandala to Karjat which, after successful execution, made Walchand's reputation as India's constructor extraordinaire. Amidst such success, this restlessly ambitious man wanted to expand elsewhere.

Impressed by reinforced cement concrete Hume pipes used for drainage and sewerage, he started the Indian Hume Pipe Company in 1931 with his brother

Ratanchand as the chief executive. In the meantime, Sir Dorabji wanted to get out of construction and offered the Tata shares to Walchand, which were bought in 1935. The company was Premier Construction—later to be Hindustan Construction Company. Not content with construction, shipping, Hume pipes and sugar (through Ravalgaon), Walchand got into two other sectors: aviation, through the Hindustan Aircraft Company, which got nationalized by the government in 1942; and automobiles, through Premier Automobiles, to manufacture passenger cars in Kurla near Bombay.

In more ways than one, Walchand was an industrialist with a difference. He was probably the greatest Indian risk-taker of his time, even more so than G.D. Birla, who was gutsy to say the least. He dared to dream big, as did Birla. He was imaginative—for who with his relatively limited cash pool could claim to build rail lines, tunnels, water supply systems, ply steamships, invest in Hume pipes, think of a car factory and even an aircraft company? He was a nationalist to core, determined to be in the vanguard of India's economic freedom. Yet he had two problems. The first was that he had a very short fuse. Second, not unlike Dwarkanath Tagore, the idea of entrepreneurship interested him more than the tedium of daily execution. This is what differentiated him from G.D. Birla, and perhaps explains why the Birlas were where they had reached in 1953, when Walchand breathed his last.

In terms of entrepreneurship, sugar was a mixed bag. Among the early managing agencies that entered this business in north India was the British firm Begg, Sutherland & Company, which pioneered the refining of *gur* without using bone charcoal to make the sugar acceptable to Hindu households. It controlled six mills in the region: Cawnpore Sugar (registered in 1894), Champarun (1905), Ryam (1913), Samastipur Central (1919), Purtabpore (1922) and Balrampur Sugar (1933). There were other British-controlled companies too, such as Belapur under W.H. Brady & Company; Belsund and United Province Sugar under James Finlay; Deccan Sugar and East India Distilleries and Sugar under E.I.D. Parry; Carew under Lyall Marshall; and Ramnuggur Cane and Sugar under Anderson Wright.[85]

Crushing cane to produce gur or molasses and then manufacturing sugar crystals was a simple enough business with low capital costs. What it needed was well-located mills to get sufficient cane from the farmers. Quite predictably, therefore, the industry soon saw an upsurge of Indian entrepreneurial interest, and the sector became even more attractive during the Depression with the advent of hefty tariff protection that eventually rose to a high 185 per cent *ad valorem*.[86]

Thus, by the 1930s, Indian-controlled sugar mill companies sprang up everywhere. Narang Brothers of Lahore founded three listed entities, with mills in Gonda, Basti and Gorakhpur in the United Provinces; Sir J.P. Srivastava set up a couple, one in Gwalior and the other in

[85] *IIYB 1945–47*, section on sugar.
[86] Bagchi (1972), p. 371.

Rampur; Ramakrishna Dalmia, a diminutive industrialist with huge drive and ruthlessness, established five in Bihar; and a relatively young man from Punjab, Karam Chand Thapar, used some of his profits from a growing coal trading and mining business in eastern India to set up a couple. Others followed, in the Bombay and Madras Presidencies.

In the first decade of the twentieth century, the average net value added from sugar manufacturing in India was less than Rs 8 million per year, compared with Rs 189 million for cotton and Rs 69 million for jute. By the second and third decade, the needle had moved a bit to under Rs 14 million and Rs 23 million per annum, respectively. The Depression and ensuing tariff protection changed things dramatically. The decadal average for the 1930s was up at Rs 63 million per year. Between 1940–41 and 1946–47 the annual average net value increased further to Rs 89 million. Sugar mills had become the fourth largest manufacturing industry in the country.[87]

Cement was of much later vintage. Despite an attempt by Bird & Company to get into this business in the late nineteenth century, there was no cement production in the country up to 1914–15. Thereafter, three relatively small-scale clinker plants, along with grinding units, came up in the limestone producing areas: Indian Cement in Porbandar managed by Tata; Katni Cement under MacDonald & Company at Katni; and Bundi Portland

[87] Sivasubraminian (2000), Table 4.17, pp. 235–36.

Cement under Killick, Nixon & Company at Bundi in Rajputana. The output was modest: till 1920, cement imports into India far exceeded production. After that, several new cement mills appeared on the scene and, by 1929, Portland cement output in India was four times that of imports.

Here Ramkrishna Dalmia played a major role. After successfully setting up his sugar mills in Bihar, he began to construct a huge cement unit in Rohtas, on the right bank of the river Sone, and had additional units coming up in Punjab, Sind and the Madras Presidency. Headstrong and individualistic, Dalmia was soon to have his skirmishes with the biggest cement company of the land—the professionally managed and widely owned Associated Cement Companies Limited (ACC), which was formed in Bombay in 1936 by a number of noted Indian industrialists and luminaries to merge the plants of four different business groups.

With units in Gujarat, Mysore, Madras, Rajputana, Central Provinces and Punjab, ACC became the giant in the industry and soon took advantage of its size and geographic spread to control supplies, and hence prices. Dalmia would have none of it, and instructed his units to unleash a fierce rate war with ACC. Eventually, a truce was hammered out in 1941 with the help of government officials. World War II created sizeable demand, and the average net value added reported by the industry rose to over Rs 25 million per year. Even so, cement was only fifth in the pecking order, following cotton, jute, iron and steel, and sugar.

Businessmen and Economic Nationalism

The Rowlatt Act of March 1919 indefinitely extended the 'emergency measures' of World War I to control public unrest and allowed the imperial government to imprison anyone suspected of terrorism for two years without trial. It created an outcry in India. Mohandas Karamchand Gandhi, back in the country from South Africa, began a nationwide strike on 6 April 1919 called the Rowlatt Satyagraha. Exactly a week later, Brigadier General Reginald Dyer ordered his Gurkha and Baluchi soldiers to shoot at a crowd that had assembled in Jallianwala Bagh, Amritsar. According to official sources, over 350 men, women and children were killed. Barbaric to the core,[88] this butchering of innocents inflamed India. Suddenly Independence became more important than before, even among some industrialists.

Among those who were strongly drawn to the call for freedom and the Mahatma were G.D. Birla and Jamnalal Bajaj. Both were very close to Gandhi and both wanted India to be free of British rule. Birla, being the most influential spokesmen for Indian business, looked at issues through the lens of commerce and economic nationalism. Jamnalal (1889–1942) was deeply and spiritually influenced by Gandhi. He transferred the management of his two businesses, the Hindustan Sugar Mills and Mukand Iron and Steel, to his son-in-law

[88] Even Winston Churchill, no great friend of Indian nationalism, called it 'monstrous', and wanted Dyer to be punished.

Rameshwar Prasad Nevatia, and dedicated the rest of his life to being a practising Gandhian.[89]

Regarding economic nationalism and the rights of Indian business, there was no champion like Birla. Having suffered barbs of the Scots and English of Calcutta, Birla did everything he could to create many fora to advance Indian interests in the country and in Britain. He helped form the Indian Chamber of Commerce in 1925, then the FICCI in 1927, which 'increasingly became the vehicle of the struggle of Indian big business against domination by European capital'.[90] An industry member of the Central Legislative Assembly, Birla fought in favour of concessions to Indian companies in coastal shipping to help Scindia Steam Navigation in its fight against Inchcape's British India Steam Navigation Company, regrettably without success. Along with Kasturbhai Lalbhai, he fought in favour of increasing protection for cotton textiles. And after the formal declaration of Purna Swaraj at the Lahore meetings of the Indian National Congress on 26 January 1930, Birla declared before the Viceroy of India in his annual presidential address to FICCI: 'I think the only solution to our present difficulties lies in strengthening the hands of those who are fighting for the freedom of our country. I have repeated it in other platforms and I

---

[89] Tripathi and Jumani (2007), p. 105. Gandhi once wrote to Birla, 'God has given me mentors . . . Among them are some of my own children, some sisters and some others like yourself and Jamnalalji who are grown-ups.' Gandhi to Birla, 20 July 1924, quoted in Kudaisya (2003), p. 91.

[90] Kudaisya (2003), p. 112

want to repeat it here again, that *Swaraj* is not a question of sentiment; it is a question of bread. The prosperity of the country depends entirely on the amount of political freedom which we get and . . . we should try to fight and strengthen the hands of those who are fighting for *Swaraj*.'[91]

Birla's frequent adviser and confidant was Sir Purshottamdas Thakurdas. A suave, low-key yet hugely well-connected cotton trader and merchant, Thakurdas was a behind-the-scenes man who intuitively knew which buttons to press to get the nationalist agenda going and when to back off. To him and Birla, economic nationalism meant capitalism that was free of the British. He also had to rein in vocal radicals like Walchand Hirachand, who wanted public fights with the government on any occasion where he thought his business interests were being circumscribed; and Kasturbhai Lalbhai who, a Gandhian to the core, fought hard but often walked out of meetings in a sulk when things were not going his way.

These then were some of the economic nationalists from the world of business: G.D. Birla, the most powerful of them, who wholly believed in freedom from colonialism while never losing sight of his business interests; Jamnalal Bajaj, beloved of the Mahatma, who gave up his day-to-day pursuit of business for the Gandhian way of life; Purshottamdas Thakurdas, a clever, sophisticated Freemason who was approachable to all and

[91] Proceedings of the Annual Meeting FICCI, 16 February 1930, quoted *ibid*., p. 125.

who, with his conciliatory and urbane body language, could quietly keep pushing the nationalist agenda of big business; Kasturbhai Lalbhai, a Gandhian to core from the 1920s, who gave up suits for khadi, and would never give up a fight for the interest of Indian, especially Ahmedabad, business; and Walchand Hirachand, who loved nothing more than to take the fight to the British and cock a snook when he could, sometimes at the expense of his own businesses.

Compared with these five, very few others from the world of business were at the frontline of the nationalist movement. Parsi businessmen were the most Westernized of the lot. They had done well under the British, faced few racial insults if any and, truth be told, were more worried about Gandhi, Nehru and the Congress than most others. Some, such as Sir Homi Mody, kowtowed to white men of appropriate position with great Anglo-Saxon finesse. Jamsetji wanted to prove a thing or two to the British and Sir Dorabji wanted to raise the banner of Tata across India, but they always did so in a polite, conciliatory way. Even J.R.D. Tata, more nationalist than many others of his kin, was too urbane, sophisticated and schooled in the ways of the West to ever raise his voice and push the rulers to the edge. Equally, Ardeshir and Pirojsha Godrej, while always in favour of Independence, were never at the forefront of organized business opposition to the raj. And this wasn't just the Parsi way of doing things. With the exception of Kasturbhai Lalbhai and Ambalal Sarabhai, the Gujarati Hindu and Jain businessmen of Ahmedabad and Bombay also preferred to stay away from nationalist politics. If they had sympathies, they weren't going to show it.

Barring Birla, Jamnalal Bajaj and, to an extent, Ramkrishna Dalmia, the Marwaris never wanted to get on the wrong side of the rulers. From Jagat Seth onwards, that was in their genes—to stick to business, operate quietly under the surface and stay out of politics. Some, such as Sir Onkarmull Jatia and Sir Badridas Goenka, prided themselves in being all-weather friends of the British managing agencies. If anything, most of the Marwari families in Calcutta and Bombay were jittery about Birla, and forever hoped that he would take his dangerous causes elsewhere.

The entrepreneurs of south India, few as they were compared with elsewhere, were quieter still. South of the Vindhyas, businessmen remained resolutely untouched by economic nationalism and the freedom movement. Whether it was the Chettiars, the brahmin entrepreneurs of Madras or the Kamma Naidus of Coimbatore, it was all about tradition, maintaining accounts, praying to the gods and keeping one's nose squeaky clean from anything that remotely resembled politics, especially of the nationalist kind.

Collieries and Tea Plantations

We are back to east India and to the primitive businesses of shovelling coal and plucking tea. From 1875 to the end of World War I, though there were some Bengali entrepreneurs in the business, the largest coalfields and mining companies were securely in the hands of British managing agencies. In 1911, for instance, eighty listed coal companies were under the British. Of these, Andrew Yule, Bird and Shaw Wallace controlled eleven each; F.W. Heilgers, which was not yet merged with Bird, controlled seven; McLeod and Macneill ran five each; and H.V. Low and Balmer Lawrie together controlled eight. There was also an Indian managing agency, N.C. Sircar & Sons, run by a Bengali, which managed seven listed coal mill companies with a combined paid-up capital of over Rs 3 million.[92] While there was little doubt about the dominance of British managing agencies in this period, it was also true that many smaller, unlisted collieries were run by wealthy Bengalis such as R.N. Bagchi, N.M. Choudhuri, S.B. Raha, B.K. Roy, Kumar Roy, R.B. Sircar, K.B. Seal and others, and accounted for a fifth of the region's pithead output.[93] Thus, the story up to 1919 was that four-fifths of India's coal output was controlled by British managing agencies, and a fifth was under smaller Indian firms.

As in jute, things started changing in coal from the mid-1920s. The industry started experiencing a nasty downturn that continued right up to the end of the Depression. Railway budgets were cut, leading to falling demand for steam-grade coal; and average pithead prices

---

[92] *IIYB 1911* and *1918*, sections on coal; and Colin P. Simmons, 'Indigenous Enterprise in the Indian Coal Mining Industry, c.1835–1939', *IESHR*, 13(2), 1976, henceforth Simmons (1976), pp. 189–90.

[93] Simmons (1976), pp. 193–95.

of coal halved compared with 1920–24 prices. The slump led to the closure of some 300 small proprietary collieries; and as many as thirty of the forty-five new joint stock collieries floated during the post-war boom period had to be liquidated. The Bengali coal baron of the time, N.C. Sircar, had to sell all his listed companies to H.V. Low & Company, after which he became a mendicant in Benares.[94]

Unlike jute, however, coal saw fewer shares changing hands in favour of Indians. In part it was because most of the collieries that collapsed were proprietary firms and had no tradable shares. More importantly, at Rs 6 lakh, the equity needs of an average colliery was a fifth of what was needed to set up a jute mill. For the same absolute outlay, British managing agents controlled well above 35 per cent of the stock of most colliery companies, whereas the proportion would have been more like 10 per cent to 15 per cent for the listed jute mills. Thus, coal companies controlled by British firms were less susceptible to creeping change of control than jute mills.[95] In 1930, therefore, 85 per cent of the listed coal companies were controlled by Europeans, and only 15 per cent by others. Even among the European-controlled collieries, only 19 per cent accommodated

---

[94] Omkar Goswami, 'Sahibs, Babus and Banias: Changes in Industrial Control in Eastern India, 1918–1950', Journal of Asian Studies, Vol. 48(2), May 1989, henceforth Goswami (1989); also reprinted in Rajat K. Ray (ed.), Entrepreneurship and Industry in India, 1800–1947, Delhi, Oxford University Press, 1992, p. 238.
[95] Ibid., p. 239.

Marwari directors, versus 59 per cent in the case of jute mill companies.[96]

However, changes began to occur from the second half of the 1930s because of the influx of Indians in the industry. Among the Marwaris were the Jatias, Ramkrishna Dalmia, Anandilal Poddar and Sukhlal Karnani who took over all the coal companies under H.V. Low, and then the Sethias, Beriwallas, Jhunjhunwallas, Bhuwalkas and Jaipurias. Karam Chand Thapar used his knowledge of the coal trade he had picked up in Calcutta to set up and acquire six collieries in the mid-1930s. Table 5 shows how the pattern of corporate control changed in the coal industry between 1942 and 1957. Even in 1942, the industry was dominantly controlled by the Europeans. By 1948, this dominance disappeared. Part of it had to do with Independence. But it was also due to Indians rushing in, either to start new coal companies or to take over the British ones.

Table 5: Changes in corporate control in listed coal companies

	1942	1945	1948	1951	1957
Indian companies	24	41	47	46	47
Companies controlled by Europeans	76	51	43	44	41
Nominally European but de facto controlled by Marwaris	0	8	10	10	12
Companies with Marwari directors	37	61	82	88	83

Source: IIYB, different years.

[96] *Ibid.*, Table 1, p. 240.

All said and done, however, mining was relatively small compared with modern manufacturing. In 1946–47, for instance, value added from factory manufacturing was Rs 2,347 million at 1938–39 prices. Mining, which included iron ore and other minerals, accounted for Rs 202 million, or under 9 per cent of factory manufacturing.[97]

Tea remained resolutely under British control throughout the colonial era and up to the 1960s. This was due to two factors. First, the more important one, every aspect of the business, from growing and nurturing the plants, plucking, drying the leaves, sorting, grading and packing to auctioning and brokering was wholly under the British. Unlike jute and coal, tea had no Indian intermediaries in the business who could have mastered the art of the trade and then got into running tea gardens. Second, some of the tea companies of consequence were sterling enterprises registered in London. This isn't to say that there were no Indian-controlled tea companies by the mid-1940s. For instance, several plantations managed by McLeod & Company had shifted to the Bajorias. However, the substantial part of the business remained white, dominated by sterling firms and large rupee companies controlled by the big British managing agencies. And well into the late 1960s, being a topi-wearing, horse-riding tea planter in Darjeeling and upper Assam, or working as a smartly suited broker and auctioneer in gora companies like J. Thomas or

[97] Sivasubramonian (2000), Table 6.10.

Carritt Moran was a heaven-sent career for many sporty brown sahib boys who graduated from Doon School, Mayo College, La Martiniere or St Xavier's College, Calcutta.

Swadeshi Bengali Businesses in East India

A fascinating story of success and failure was that of the swadeshi Bengali enterprises of east India. After Curzon's partitioning of Bengal in 1905, and in response to the call of the scientifically driven entrepreneurial nationalism of Prafulla Chandra Ray and Jagdish Chandra Bose, Bengal saw a burst of modern enterprises. The province already had some cotton textile mills under Bengali ownership and control. To these were added more modern establishments such as Bengal Chemicals and Pharmaceuticals for drugs and medicines, founded by Bose and Ray and run by a scientist, litterateur and a renaissance-like personality called Rajsekhar Bose; Calcutta Chemicals, which was started by two families, the Mitras and the Dasguptas, to manufacture soap, toothpaste and herbal cosmetics; Bengal Lamps, promoted by Kiran Shankar Roy, a zamindar and Congress politician educated in New College, Oxford, for making electric bulbs; and Bengal Immunity for vaccines. There was also Bengal Pottery Works, owned by Manindra Chandra Nundy, the Maharaja of Kasimbazar; then the Dutt-family founded Comilla Bank, which later became United Bank of India; and two major newspaper groups—the *Ananda Bazar* owned by the Sarkars, and the

Amrita Bazar–Jugantar–Dainik Basumati group owned by the Ghosh family.[98]

Most of these companies did well up to the mid-1930s. There was a growing demand for their goods among the urban middle class, and these firms regularly advertised in the Bengali newspapers to induce consumers to buy modern products made by swadeshi Bengali enterprise. Besides, there was no competition worth the name. Neither were the British managing agencies interested in such businesses, nor had the multinational corporations (MNCs) come into the fray. Unfortunately, things changed for the worse by the late 1930s and 1940s. Some of it had to do with the seemingly congenital inability of Bengalis to run businesses: there were squabbles between partners that only got worse, litigations, and sons and relatives turning out to be profoundly inept managers. But this was only partly true.

There were two more significant reasons. Most of the Bengali enterprises were closely held, with relatively low equity base. They were closely held because of the promoters' desire to maintain their 'Bengali-ness'. And they were parsimoniously capitalized because funds were hard to come by for non-European, non-traders like the Bengalis during 1905–1918, when many of these firms were founded. Steady growth for these companies, especially for the ones needing technologically advanced machines and testing equipment, called for funds. That

[98] This section is almost entirely from Goswami (1989).

could be managed either by re-ploughing most, if not all, of the profits back into the enterprises; or by issuing fresh equity to the public. The Bengali promoters hardly ever did the former, for they demanded their wealth in dividends. And they would not countenance the latter lest their companies should be taken over by the Marwaris, whom the Bengalis detested far more than they did the British. So, over time, these once technologically superior companies got into severe cash binds, which choked off their growth.

A more damaging blow was delivered by the MNCs. By the late 1930s, Lifebuoy and Sunlight soap sold by Lever Brothers had captured a sizeable segment of the Indian soap market, much to the detriment of Calcutta Chemicals—which also faced competition from Colgate-Palmolive for toothpastes.[99] Bengal Lamp was being challenged by the products of General Electric Company and then Philips (India) Limited. Local biscuit makers like Kolay & Sons were facing competition from Britannia Biscuits, a wholly owned subsidiary of Britain's Associated Biscuit Manufacturers.

---

[99] The competition was severe enough for Hari Shankar Paul of the Indian Soap Manufacturers' Association to complain that powerful, wholly foreign-owned companies with huge paid-up capital, low cost technologies, higher scale of operations and large marketing outlays were driving the smaller patriotic Indian soap makers from the market (*Hindustan Standard*, 1 January 1938). Paul was correct. The paid-up capital of Lever Brothers was Rs 88 lakh—way higher than what Calcutta Chemicals or Godrej Soaps could have ever dreamt of.

Thus, most of the Bengali swadeshi enterprises were squeezed from both ends: the relative lack of capital to expand fast enough, and intense competition from MNCs, who had much deeper pockets and were in for a long haul.[100]

Whatever Happened in the South?

During the period of heady entrepreneurial growth throughout most of India, often couched in the language of economic nationalism, the south seemed to belong to an altogether different world. Despite the growth of spinning mills in the 1930s in Coimbatore, thanks to the energy of the Kamma Naidus, and the establishment of the Indian Bank in 1907, Madras Presidency had little to show in terms of modern Indian capitalistic enterprise.

It need not have been like that. The nineteenth century had seen some remarkable entrepreneurial moves in the region, albeit by the British. William Dare, who became the head of Parry & Company after the death of Thomas Parry, got the firm involved in various activities:

[100] The one swadeshi business that escaped being caught in a pincer was printed news. The market continued to expand and there was no competition from anything resembling an MNC or even a Bennett Coleman of our times. The *Amrita Bazar–Jugantar–Dainik Basumati* group survived till the early 1970s, only to fail because of internal squabbles of the Ghosh family. The *Ananda Bazar* group continues to this day, much larger and financially stronger than ever before.

coffee plantations in Mysore, sugar mills and distilleries in South Arcot, fertilizers, sulphuric acid and a pottery work at Ranipettai called 'The Pottery', which later produced what we now know as Parryware. The other Madras-based giant was Binny & Company, originally in the agency business and coastal trade, which founded the Buckingham Mill in 1876 and the Carnatic Mill in 1881, and then acquired the managing agency of the Bangalore Woollen, Cotton and Silk Mills in 1886. Then there was A. and F. Harvey & Company, which promoted the Tinnevely Mills at Ambasamudram (1883), the Coral Mills in Tuticorin (1887) and the largest of them all, the Madura Mill (1892) at Madurai to produce yarn and, later, sewing thread. T. Stains & Company collaborated with another managing agency, Arbuthnot & Company, to set up the Coimbatore Spinning and Weaving Company in 1888.[101]

Despite such industrial initiatives by the British, few if any Indians in the south, barring the Kamma Naidus of Coimbatore, got into any manufacturing for the first four decades of the twentieth century. And it wasn't for dearth of private capital. The Chettiars, for instance, had plenty of capital, but preferred to be in trade and moneylending. The wealthiest of them all, A.M. Murugappa Chettiar, gave up his rice trade and moneylending business in Burma and south-east Asia after losing a fortune in 1929–30 to return to Madras where he restarted from scratch. He got into abrasives in the 1940s, but not much else.

[101] Tripathi and Jumani (2007), pp. 71–2.

Today, the Murugappa group is in various sectors, from steel tubes and cycles to fertilizers, abrasives, sugar and general insurance. Most of these ventures, however, were forays made after Independence—sometimes much after. Other Chettiars also entered industry in the 1940s, mostly in cotton textiles, but they proceeded very gingerly, without the dash or verve of the Indian business families in the west, the east or the north.

If anything, the brahmins of Madras were even more circumspect. After spending years as an accountant, a company secretary and then as the first Indian full-time director of a well-known, Madras-based, British-controlled company called Simpson, Sivasailam Anantharamakrishnan, a brahmin from Tirunelveli district, eventually took over the enterprise in 1941, which then became the Amalgamated group. Its initial interests were in publishing, but it later branched out into automobile forgings and ancillaries, mostly after Independence. T.V. Sundaram Iyengar started his business journey in 1911 as a provider of rural transport services in parts of the Madras Presidency. Though the TVS group is very large today in the automobile industry, it had little in terms of manufacturing at the time of Independence. In 1928, T.T. Krishnamachari, later a disgraced finance minister under Jawaharlal Nehru, started the TTK group, which began manufacturing kitchen utensils. Its famously ubiquitous Prestige household pressure cooker came much later.

In truth, there were only two Tamil brahmins who entered industry during the period 1919–47. Two siblings started the eponymous Seshasayee Brothers, which became reputed in design and construction of electrical substations; they set up three companies in different parts of the Madras Presidency to bid for electrification projects. The other was C. Rajan Iyer, a steel dealer in south India, who used the profits he made during World War I to promote the Indian Steel Rolling Mills in 1934.[102]

It is a fascinating question why south India, barring Coimbatore, was such an outlier. There was no dearth of wealth in the city of Madras, in the major rice growing districts of the Presidency, in Travancore and Cochin, in the kingdom of Mysore, in the Telugu-speaking, anicut canal-irrigated wet districts of Krishna, West and East Godavari and in the Nizam's territory. Yet there was relatively little industrialization right up to the early 1960s. A somewhat related question is why most of south India stayed away from mainstream nationalism, right from the Rowlatt Satyagraha in 1919 to the Quit India movement in 1942. The honest answer to both questions is probably sociological and cultural. Whatever the answer, it needs investigation.

Corporate India, 1900–01 versus 1946–47

It is time now for a synoptic view of India's industrialization between 1900–01 and 1946–47. In 1900–01, India's real GDP was Rs 16,303 million (or Rs 1,630 crore), of which the share of the primary sector was 60.5 per

[102] *Ibid.*, p. 107.

cent. The entire secondary sector, consisting of mining, factory-based manufacturing and small-scale and cottage industries, added up to Rs 1,857 million, or 11.4 per cent of GDP. Value added from modern factories was tinier still, at Rs 322 million or 2 per cent of GDP, small-scale and cottage industries producing over four times more output.

Fast-forward to 1946–47. Real GDP had risen to Rs 26,290 million (Rs 2,629 crore). At an exponential trend rate of just 1 per cent per year, it was not a particularly impressive growth over the period. However, within this milieu of limited growth, both the secondary sector and factory manufacturing did well for themselves. The former grew at 1.7 per cent per annum; and output from factory manufacturing rose at a trend rate of 3.7 per cent per year. Simply put, over the period, year on year, value added produced by India's factories increased at a rate 3.7 times that of the country's real GDP. This is something worth remembering, for it had much to do with the native entrepreneurial energy that India witnessed through the second half of the period. Consequently, the structure of national output changed—perhaps not dramatically, but significantly enough to be noticeable.

The share of the primary sector—comprising agriculture, forestry, fishing and plantations—fell steadily, from 60.5 per cent of GDP in 1900–01 to 46.2 per cent in 1946–47. Within the secondary sector, the share of small-scale and cottage industries reduced modestly, from 8.8 per cent in the beginning of the era to 6.8 per cent at Independence. The most stellar growth was in modern manufacturing, whose share rose from 2 per cent of GDP in 1900–01 to 8.9 per cent in 1946–47. Indeed, it would have been over 10 per cent—as it had been a year earlier—had manufacturing not suffered from the uncertainties of Partition in 1946–47. By any yardstick, it was a brilliant performance, the more so for happening in a poor colonial nation where per capita GDP had grown by less than 10 per cent over forty-seven years. Credit for much of this growth lay with Indian entrepreneurs, whatever industry they were in, whether it was cotton textiles, jute, iron and steel, sugar or cement. They braved the odds to build the industrial sinews of modern India, which was to be further worked upon after Independence.

Numbers often speak louder than words. Table 6 contains data on the control of publicly listed companies by British and Indian managing agencies across various industries at the time of Independence. It shows that in tea the British were firmly in control, which was to continue well into the 1960s; in jute, while they continued to rule, Indians had definitely got into their domain and would accelerate the process through takeovers in the 1950s; in cotton, which was very much an Indian-dominated industry, as was sugar and even electric supply and engineering—both technologically more complex than the others—more listed companies were controlled by Indian managing agencies than British. Indian entrepreneurship had come to stay.

Table 6: Span of control of British and Indian managing agencies, c. 1947

Listed companies in	Controlled by	
	British managing agencies	Indian managing agencies
Collieries	28	20
Jute	48	11
Tea	113	11
Cotton	15	47
Sugar	6	19
Electricity	13	15
Engineering	10	15
Miscellaneous	63	60
Total	296	198

Source: IIYB 1945–47 and 1952.

An amazing feature of the seventy-two-year period from 1875 to 1947 covered in this chapter was the fidelity of one organizational form—that of the managing agency. Records of individual companies listed in the *Investor's India Year Book* from 1911 to 1947 demonstrate that barring banks and some insurance companies, hardly any firms operated outside this arrangement. In an era where entrepreneurship was scarce and capital difficult to garner, businessmen preferred an organizational structure that gave them corporate control over their ventures with relatively little ownership and helped spread risks across different commercial activities. Through their share of revenue, profits and various other contracts, the system also gave them access to additional rewards for risk taking—greater than mere dividends, which the man in the street got in the same proportion as the promoter. Thus, managing agencies continued to flourish unabatedly through the period, as they would well after the Union Jack came down.

4

1947–1970: CONTROLLED, SHRUNK AND FINISHED

By the second half of the 1930s, any Indian businessman of consequence knew what Jawaharlal Nehru stood for. It was no secret, for Nehru's views on the desirable political economy and society of independent India were in the public domain. Captivated by the seeming success of the Soviet Union, Nehru made it amply clear that he stood for a '[planned] economy based on socialist principles' and wanted to put an end to 'all special class privileges and vested interests'.[103] He began his presidential speech at the Lucknow session of the Indian National Congress in April 1936 by addressing the Congressmen as 'Comrades';

---

[103] Jawaharlal Nehru, *Glimpses of World History*, Allahabad, 1934–35, reprinted Delhi 2004; quoted in Rudrangshu Mukherjee, *Nehru & Bose: Parallel Lives*, Penguin/Viking, 2014, henceforth Mukherjee (2014), pp. 106–07.

spoke of how 'in the Soviet territories, a new conception of human freedom and social equality [is] being fought desperately against a host of enemies'; how socialism was 'a philosophy of life . . . a vital creed'; why the Congress should become a socialist organization; and why rapid industrialization under the rubric of socialism was the only way to eradicate mass poverty in India. He even saw Gandhi's beloved khadi and village industries as merely 'temporary expedients of a transition stage rather than as solutions to our vital problems'.[104]

Indian capitalists were alarmed. Here was Nehru, Gandhi's favourite, destined to lead a soon-to-be independent nation, who was a firm supporter of socialism and behaved as if he despised the world of business.[105] In May 1936, a month after the Lucknow session, a group of twenty-one important Bombay businessmen signed a toughly worded manifesto against the Congress president. Without naming Nehru, the well-publicized document declared that the signatories 'are unequivocally opposed to ideas of this kind being propagated . . . [and] are convinced [that] there is a grave risk of the masses of the country being misled by such doctrines into believing that all that is required for the improvement of their well-being

[104] Mukherjee (2014), *ibid*., pp. 141–43.
[105] It mattered little to most of them that all the leftist-socialist resolutions proposed in Lucknow were defeated, and that Gandhi cleverly constrained Nehru's proletarian sympathies by packing the Congress Working Committee with centrists and right wingers such as C. Rajagopalachari, Rajendra Prasad and Vallabhbhai Patel.

is a total destruction of the existing social and economic structure.'[106] The signatories were knighted heavyweights such as Sir Purshottamdas Thakurdas, Sir Chunilal Mehta, Sir Ardeshir Dalal, Sir V.N. Chandavarkar, Sir Homi Mody, Sir Cowasji Jehangir and Sir Chimanlal Setalvad.

Though wary of Nehru, G.D. Birla, by virtue of his closeness to Gandhi and the Congress, was more aware of the limitations of Jawaharlal's writ in an era of the Mahatma. He, therefore, castigated Purshottamdas Thakurdas by writing, 'I am surprised that you should put your name to a document the contents of which . . . were liable to be seriously misinterpreted'; and with Walchand Hirachand he was tougher still: 'You have rendered no service to your caste men. It is curious how we businessmen are so shortsighted. It looks very crude for a man of property to say that he is opposed to expropriation in the wider interest of the country.' At that point, Birla felt that 'Socialism is only another name for the impatience of Jawaharlal', and expected it to be significantly tempered by the necessities of realpolitik. Perspicacious on most matters, how wrong Birla was on this![107]

The Bombay Plan of 1944

Given the typical businessman's aversion to socialism and his concerns about Nehru becoming the first prime minister of independent India, it is strange but true that

---

[106] Kudaisya (2003), p. 169.
[107] *Ibid.*, pp. 169–70.

some leading lights of the corporate world came up with a document in January 1944 called the Bombay Plan. Titled *A Brief Memorandum Outlining a Plan of Economic Development for India*, its signatories were: (i) Jehangir Ratanji Dadabhoy (J.R.D.) Tata, then all of forty and chairman of Tata Sons for the last six years, (ii) G.D. Birla, (iii) Sir Ardeshir Dalal, ex-ICS and on the board of several Tata group companies, (iv) Lala Shri Ram, (v) Kasturbhai Lalbhai, (vi) Ardeshir Darabshaw Shroff, an economist who later became the chairman of Bank of India and New India Assurance Company, and later founded the Forum of Free Enterprise as a counter to Nehruvian socialism, (vii) Sir Purshottamdas Thakurdas and (viii) John Mathai, an economist and member-secretary of the group, who became independent India's first railways minister and also served as the minister of finance.[108]

The idea of the Bombay Plan was to present a 'reasoned' alternative to populist socialism that the authors feared might overtake decision making after Independence, especially if there were loud political demands for income and wealth redistribution. They believed that making the powers-to-be and the English-speaking intelligentsia aware of an orderly path of post-colonial development could help nip nascent socialist tendencies in the bud.[109]

---

[108] Three of the eight worthies—Ardeshir Dalal, Ardeshir Shroff and Purshottamdas Thakurdas—were also signatories to the note of 1936 which had publicly castigated Nehru for leading the Congress along a socialist path of development.

[109] Amal Sanyal, 'The Curious Case of the Bombay Plan', *Contemporary Issues and Ideas in Social Sciences*, June 2010, mimeo,

There was another unspoken objective. The members knew of the admiration that many Indian politicians had for the success of the Soviet Union in prevailing upon Nazi Germany, and anticipated the coming of state planning in some form or the other after Independence. Given these expectations, the Bombay Planners thought it would be better for industry to be perceived as a trusted partner in planned progress than as being churlishly opposed to government intervention in the nation's economic affairs.

In fact, the advent of World War II had already sowed the seeds of widespread state intervention in the nation's economic and business affairs. Much of the controls and regulations that India was to groan under in the late 1950s, 1960s and 1970s emerged out of the Defence of India Act, 1939, and its accompanying rules. For instance, Rule 81 of the Defence of India rules created a blanket provision for 'regulating or prohibiting the production, treatment, keeping, storage, movement, transport, distribution, disposal, acquisition, use or consumption of articles or things of any description whatsoever'; and for 'controlling the prices (or rates) at which articles or things of any description whatsoever may be sold'. The same rule allowed the government to set up 'controllers to exercise control over the pricing and distribution of supplies and services essential to the life of the community'. There were other diktats as well—such as giving power to the

---

p. 6, quoting correspondence between John Mathai and Purshottamdas Thakurdas from the Purshottamdas Thakurdas Papers, Nehru Memorial Museum and Library.

government to control access to foreign currencies.[110] Thus, with the tea leaves getting arranged to forecast the advent of central planning, capitalists such as J.R.D. Tata, Birla, Lala Shri Ram and Kasturbhai Lalbhai wanted, through the Bombay Plan, to publicize the views of responsible nationalist businessmen in fashioning the growth of independent India.

It was a fifteen-year plan with the objective of attaining for all citizens 'a general standard of living which would leave a reasonable margin over the minimum requirements of human life'. For this to happen, per capita real income needed to double over the period. And since the population was growing at 5 million per year, national income had to treble in fifteen years. This needed a 130 per cent increase in agricultural output, a 500 per cent growth in industry and a doubling of income from services. In effect, the Bombay Plan made a case for structural transformation of the nation's economy. If everything worked as outlined in the plan, the composition of GDP would change dramatically, with the share of agriculture dropping to 40 per cent; of industry rising to 35 per cent; and of services to 25 per cent. The capital outlay over fifteen years was Rs 10,000 crore (Rs 100 billion) or $30 billion at the exchange rate of the time.[111]

---

[110] Rakesh Mohan and Vandana Aggarwal, 'Commands and Control: Planning for Indian Industrial Development, 1951–1990', *Journal of Comparative Economics*, Vol. 14, 1990, pp. 683–84.

[111] Sanyal (2010), pp. 9–10. The base year numbers are different from Sivasubramonian's calculations because these were from

This is no place to delve into the intricacies of the Bombay Plan. What needs emphasizing is how a group of private businessmen was making a powerful case for deficit financing and for an overarching role for the central government. Some questions naturally arise. Why did industrialists with their apparently visceral aversion to socialism make such a strong case for central planning and the predominance of government in India's postcolonial economic life? Was it economic nationalism on the part of men who, while being in industry, were known for their commitment to the public weal? Or was it self-seeking, in the hope that deficit-financed government investment would lift economic activity to point after which profit-driven capitalists and business houses could take over? Or was the plan delusionary, the industrialists not realizing the strength of Nehru's and his followers' resolve to see their socialist vision through?

It wasn't delusion on the part of the industrialists. Despite the rising tide of socialism within the Congress, one must remember that the Bombay Plan was drafted when the party had quite a few pro-business, right-of-centre leaders who had the seniority and gravitas to take on Nehru and the left wing—starting with Gandhi, who was anything but a socialist, and buttressed by people such as Rajagopalachari, Vallabhbhai Patel and Rajendra Prasad. The authors of the plan were not expected to know

---

V.K.R.V. Rao's national income estimate of 1931–32 that was pushed out to 1943–44.

that Gandhi would be assassinated four years later, that Patel was to die in December 1950, that Rajagopalachari would effectively exile himself from the thrust and parry of national politics, or that Prasad would be the first President of the country and so occupy a Constitutional position of de facto silence, leaving the field open for Nehru and his socialist young Turks.

Nor was the plan self-seeking. While none of the eight members could be remotely described as a votary of socialism, each was an advocate of planned industrialization and economic development. A balanced view of why profit-driven capitalists who drafted such a document must necessarily incorporate the role of nationalism. Each member wanted an independent India and, together, they wanted a rational, mixed economy where the state would provide an umbrella under which private enterprise could grow and flourish. In the context of the 1940s, this was neither a radical thought nor a self-seeking stratagem as the communists made it out to be. Instead, it was making the case for a wider nationalist platform where a modern, forward-looking, newly decolonized state would actively cooperate with the world of business to jointly create the much-needed industrial capital of the nation.

The State of Play in 1947

The Partition was an unconscionable tragedy. There was no official count, but anywhere between 500,000 to a million children, women and men were butchered in a few months' time. Over 14 million people had their lives and homes uprooted as they trudged to India or Pakistan. Another four million followed in the early 1950s from East Pakistan to eke out a miserable existence in slums that sprung up in and around Calcutta and eastern India. The sheer violence of the Partition, coupled with Pakistan's incursion into Kashmir in 1948 and its annexation of the western parts of the Valley, created another catastrophe. This one was economic, for it extinguished all hopes of business or commercial cooperation between the two nations.

Although some Indian industrialists, including G.D. Birla and Bajaj, lost factories and facilities with the split, India was distinctly better off than Pakistan in terms of the balance of business interests.[112] Contemporary analysis by Professor C.N. Vakil, a distinguished economist of the time, showed that over 90 per cent of the total industrial establishments of the undivided subcontinent remained within India; as did 95 per cent of total electricity generation; and 89 per cent of joint stock companies representing 97 per cent of the total paid-up capital. Table 7 gives a sense of how much better off India was vis-à-vis Pakistan after Partition.

[112] The Birlas lost the Sutlej Cotton Mills in Lahore, as did Lala Shri Ram the Lyallpur Cotton Mills. So, too, did the Bajaj group, then under Kamalnayan Bajaj after the death of Jamnalal in 1942, which lost the original Mukand Iron and Steel Company.

Table 7: How industries were split with the Partition

Industries	India	Pakistan	Share of India
	Number of units		
Cotton Mills	380	14	96%
Jute Mills	108	0	100%
Sugar Mills	166	10	94%
Cement Mills	19	6	76%
Engineering	1,734	278	86%
Heavy Chemicals	38	2	95%
Iron and Steel	18	0	100%
Paper Mills	49	0	100%

Source: C.N. Vakil, *Economic Consequences of Divided India: A Study of the Economy of India and Pakistan* (Bombay 1950).

For all its regional inequalities, India after 1947 was clearly well placed to pursue a path of fairly rapid economic development led by private capital. Most of the industrial establishments remained within the country, as did the banks and stock exchanges. Barring Karachi and to a lesser extent Chittagong, the major ports were in India. The bulk of electricity generation and distribution was also with India. It got 85 per cent of the railway tracks too, and the same share of locomotives and goods wagons. And, most important, it retained the vast majority of Indian entrepreneurial families who had created the first wave of industrialization during the initial four decades of the twentieth century.

Therefore, in terms of entrepreneurial capital, physical infrastructure, financial wherewithal, legal framework and the sheer weight of industrial activity,

India was certainly the best-off decolonized nation of the time. This ought to have set the stage for healthy growth of a mixed economy, with private industry leading the charge wherever possible and the state contributing in setting up large-scale enterprises as well as education, social development and activities that had significant externalities and economies of scale. Unfortunately, that didn't happen. By 1956, the country saw the beginnings of a state-led control economy with a concomitant bureaucratic structure that grew unchallenged over the passing years, eventually leaving India far behind where it could have been.

Managing Agencies Still Ruled the Roost

In the early 1950s, private business houses and their managing agencies were very much in control of their world. The *Investor's India Year Book, 1952*, after pronouncing, 'It is emphatically not the function of the state itself to undertake the process of manufacture and production. Its role is that of a referee to see that the play is fair and the rules observed', went on to give data that showed the extent of managing agency control across all key industries.

East India was still the domain of British managing agents, though Indians were hot on their tail in coal and jute. In 1950–51, there were forty-nine listed coal companies, of which twenty-seven were run by British managing agencies, twenty-one by Indians, and one by B.N. Elias & Company, an old Calcutta-based Armenian business house. Despite rapid Indian entry, the British still controlled the larger coalfields and accounted for 76 per cent of total sales, versus 23 per cent for the Indians. There were seven collieries under Andrew Yule & Company that together notched up sales worth almost Rs 70 million, and of which one, the Bengal Coal Company, was huge, having rights over 55,000 acres of rich, coal-bearing land and generating a revenue of Rs 56 million. Bird and Heilgers together controlled nine coal companies accounting for Rs 48 million in sales. Macneill & Barry managed four collieries that earned total revenue of over Rs 49 million, with one company, Equitable Coal, earning revenue of almost Rs 40 million. And Shaw Wallace controlled three coal companies that together earned a revenue of over Rs 20 million.[113]

In jute too, despite the growing presence of mills controlled by Marwaris, the British managing agencies were very much in the forefront in 1950–51. Of the sixty listed jute mill companies, forty-eight remained under British managing agencies and accounted for Rs 87.5 million in manufacturing profits; and eleven under Marwari managing agencies earned profits of over Rs 38 million.[114] Bird and Heilgers together controlled ten jute mill companies; McLeod managed nine; Andrew Yule's

[113] *Investor's India Year Book (IIYB), 1952*, section on coal.
[114] As in collieries, one was managed by B.N. Elias and Company. For some strange reason, the *IIYB 1952* data on jute mills do not give the sales figures. Instead, these start with manufacturing profits, which are akin to today's earnings before interest, taxes, depreciation and amortisation (EBITDA).

writ ran over eight; Jardine Henderson had six; Macneill & Barry had four; Thomas Duff controlled three sterling companies whose shares were traded in Calcutta; and Mackinnon Mackenzie, Kettlewell Bullen and Gillanders Arbuthnot controlled a brace each.[115]

There were, of course, several other, smaller, unlisted jute mill companies and collieries that were under Indian ownership and control. Two things are worth noting. First, as discussed in Chapter 3, the first five years, indeed a decade, after Independence saw no great change in the pattern of corporate control. No doubt, with the tricolour flying, Indian entrepreneurial groups were more visible in jute and coal than earlier. Yet there was neither any clearly obvious sign of retreat by the British managing agencies, nor a more determined advance of the Indians into Calcutta's Anglo-Saxon business citadels than what occurred in the 1930s and 1940s. That was to come later.

Second, the British-run companies were beginning to look like a tired lot. In jute, for instance, despite facing identical market conditions, the forty-eight mill companies controlled by British managing agencies earned an average profit of Rs 1.8 million per enterprise in 1950–51, versus Rs 3.5 million per company run by the Marwari agencies.[116] After seventy-five years of running the show in east India, the old jute and coal sahibs of

[115] *IIYB 1952*, section on jute mills.
[116] It is possible that some of the British managing agencies, believing that their days were numbered, siphoned off extra profits as various forms of commission and fees. This cannot be proven one way or the other from the data. Casual evidence

Dalhousie Square were starting to behave as if they were getting ready to pack their bags. As a partner in Calcutta's leading solicitor firm Orr Dignam & Company observed, the managing agencies 'were not initiating, they were just managing . . . they were not planning beyond the point when they would go back home'.[117]

It was vastly different in tea, especially among the listed companies, where British managing agencies ruled in no uncertain terms. All said and done, this was a business closely controlled and monopolized at all levels by the white man. Tea was grown in plantations run by the British; it was sold through British-run auction houses in Calcutta and exported to buyers and markets that the expatriates knew only too well. There were no native intermediaries as in jute or coal. Expatriate control was total; and industry knowledge remained within a close community. For these reasons the expatriate enclave ruled this industry much longer than it did others.

The facts bear this out. In 1950, there were 124 listed rupee tea companies whose shares were quoted on the Calcutta Stock Exchange. Of these, 113 were under British managing agencies; they ranged from giant estates in Assam like Hasimara, Patrakhola and Bishnauth to much smaller ones in Cachar and the Dooars, and accounted for 95 per cent of the 1.25 million maunds (46.6 million kg) of tea produced in India. Duncan Brothers

----

seems to suggest that the Marwaris were far superior in squeezing costs and managing working capital than the Britons.

[117] H.C. Waters, quoted in Jones (1992), p. 2.

was at the top, controlling twenty-four such companies and supplying 23 per cent of the tea grown in 1950. Then came Andrew Yule, which had fourteen companies accounting for 11 per cent of the produce. McLeod also had fourteen companies in its stable and produced 10 per cent of India's tea. Williamson Magor and Octavius Steel controlled twelve firms each, with the former supplying 10 per cent of the total output and the latter 8 per cent. Tea was, therefore, not only overwhelmingly white but also highly concentrated—with five British managing agencies controlling 61 per cent of the rupee companies and 62 per cent of the industry's output.[118]

Cotton textile mills across India were dominated by Indian entrepreneurs and their managing agencies, though there were some British-controlled mills in Bombay and the Madras Presidency. That too didn't change immediately after Independence. In 1950–51, forty-seven of the sixty-two listed cotton mill companies were under the control of Indian managing agencies and accounted for 69 per cent of total profits of the industry. The British managed fifteen, which generated 31 per cent of profits.[119]

---

[118] *IIYB 1952*, section on tea. This data does not incorporate the size of the large sterling companies for the want of precise comparability. If that were done, British dominance in the early 1950s would be greater still.

[119] There was, however, an episode of government intervention which, to the perspicacious might have given a foretaste of things to come. Thanks to mismanagement, Sholapur Spinning and Weaving, a mill controlled by an Indian managing agency Morarka & Company had posted large losses for three consecutive years, 1948, 1949 and 1950. In

In sugar, six of the twenty-five listed enterprises were still under British control, the remaining nineteen being run by Indian managing agencies. In engineering, British managing agencies ran the affairs of ten of the twenty-five listed companies in 1950–51, but their share in the total profits of these enterprises was only 28 per cent. Thanks to the overwhelming presence of a single Indian giant, the Tata Iron and Steel Company (TISCO), the fifteen firms controlled by Indian managing agencies accounted for 72 per cent of the profits.

So far as other listed companies covering a wide range of sectors were concerned—they were labelled under the head 'miscellaneous' in successive *IIYB*s—things looked very evenly balanced in 1950–51. Of the 123 companies in this category, sixty-three were under British control and sixty under Indians.

Notwithstanding many similarities in structure and form in the relationships between managing agents and their companies, there were three notable differences between the British agencies in Calcutta that controlled jute, tea and coal in the eastern part of the country and their Indian counterparts in Bombay, Ahmedabad, Kanpur and Delhi, who were into cotton, sugar and miscellaneous enterprises. One was the span of control. The larger managing agencies in Calcutta

response, the Government of India passed an ordinance in 1950 that immediately suspended the managing agency and appointed a new board of directors under the chairmanship of Sir V.N. Chandavarkar. It was an early episode of direct state intervention in the affairs of privately run companies.

had considerable heft. Even in the early 1950s, when the empire was a thing of the past, Andrew Yule managed forty listed companies; the Bird-Heilgers group thirty; Jardine fifteen; McLeod and Duncan Brothers twenty-four each; Octavius Steel twenty-two; and Gillanders Arbuthnot fourteen. In contrast, with the exception of the Tatas and Birla Brothers, each of whom controlled eleven large listed companies—and also to an extent Kasturbhai Lalbhai and Dalmia Sahu Jain—most of the Indian agencies managed far fewer enterprises. In cotton textiles, for instance, barring the Tatas and Birla who had ten mill companies each under them and Kasturbhai who had six, Indians controlled one to three mills each, with many having just one.[120]

Why so? That raises the second difference: the distinct disparity in the financial might between the large British managing agencies of Calcutta and, excluding the Tatas and Birla, most Indian managing agencies in eastern India and elsewhere. By virtue of investing in several different industries with diverse cash flows, the British in Calcutta had more internal accruals at their disposal than most native Indians—which they used to strengthen their hold in each sector and also to expand their span of control. In contrast, most of the Indian managing agencies in Bombay and Ahmedabad stuck to one sector, usually cotton, occasionally buttressed by sugar. They were consequently limited by the extent of free cash that they had which, in turn, either restricted their forays into other industries or

[120] *IIYB, 1951.*

did not allow them steady consolidation by setting up and buying out mills.[121]

The third difference had to do with holding power. Thanks to their control over a large number of companies, the bigger British managing agencies of Calcutta (and the Tatas and Birla Brothers) could withstand financial downturns without being forced to sell their enterprises to others—as happened in large measure during the Depression. The smaller agencies, which controlled just a few enterprises, often in one or two industries, could not endure this. Financial shocks over two or three years or insoluble family disagreements often forced them to cash out and sell their companies to other managing agents. That was what happened quite frequently in Bombay and Ahmedabad, which saw a much greater churn in controlling rights among Indian managing agencies than did Calcutta up to the early 1950s.

One significant change, though in its early-stage, had begun to show up in the corporate world: the advent of the 'India Limited' companies of major multinationals. This will be discussed a bit later. But it is worth noting that even in 1950–51, Imperial Chemical Industries of the UK had listed an Indian subsidiary, the Alkali and Chemical Corporation of India; Dunlop had set up Dunlop Rubber (India) Limited, whose shares were publicly traded. And there were the listed Metal Box (India) Limited and

---

[121] Thus, for instance, in coal and jute alone in 1950–51, the listed companies controlled by Andrew Yule earned Rs 2.5 crore of distributable profits, and the Bird-Heilgers group netted Rs 2 crore. *Ibid.*, sections on jute and coal.

Indian Aluminium, a subsidiary of Aluminium Company of Canada, or Alcan. Soon these companies and others were to play a significant role in corporate India.

Thus, cataclysmic as it may have been in political and human terms, India's independence did not immediately result in an exodus of expatriate firms. So far as the balance of corporate control between Indian and British managing agencies was concerned, little if anything changed up to the late 1950s or the early 1960s.

There were, however, some winds of change in corporate law regarding the power of managing agencies, which began over a decade earlier with the Indian Companies (Amendment) Act of 1936. For instance, the law demanded a statutory annual statement of any public limited company signed by the chairman or at least two directors, which had to be considerably more transparent about the enterprise's financial relationships with its managing agents than before. It eliminated the practice of any company having a contract with its managing agency in perpetuity and, instead, put a cap of no more than twenty years for such contracts; it forbade companies from making loans to their managing agents, and forbade two companies under the same managing agent from transacting in shares and debentures with each other; it limited commissions to managing agencies to a fixed percentage of annual net profits; and, unless passed by four-fifths of the directors, prohibited any future contracts of a company with its managing agency that involved sales, purchase and supply of goods and material. These were irritants for the agencies, especially after decades of enjoying a free reign. But, truth be told, there were enough provisos in the 1936 statute to thwart any major hurdles to the financial benefits that accrued to the managing agencies.

To be sure, by the mid-1950s, some British promoters and managers were perceptive enough to grasp that their years were numbered. Yet nothing really changed in the commercial hubs of Bombay, Calcutta or Madras. The Bengal Club was still 'whites only' in substance, as was the Calcutta Swimming Club. Alipore was overwhelmingly white, as were the tiny tots in Miss Higgins School. Leisurely lunches were still eaten by sahibs in the large dining rooms of their offices. Yes, India had become independent and got its own Constitution, and Dickie Mountbatten had returned home with Edwina. But, really, what had changed in Park Street and the Calcutta Cricket and Football Club?

Creating the Commanding Heights, 1951 to 1964

Far removed from the rattan-chaired drinking holes of white planters in Assam, in the Dooars and in the expatriate clubs of Calcutta, what began to change was the speed with which an ex-Harrovian and graduate in natural sciences from Trinity College, Cambridge was trying to bring in a more socialist order of things. Jawaharlal Nehru was clear about his vision for independent India—one with less poverty and inequality, and a polity driven by egalitarian socialism. This, he believed, needed much greater state direction, an era of centralized planning, and growing public ownership of the means of production.

On 6 April 1948, seven months and a few days after Independence, the nation still without a Constitution and in dominion status, Nehru's government announced an industrial policy resolution. It emphasized the need for India to grow rapidly and do so with a more equitable distribution of income and wealth which, it believed, was possible only if the state played a progressively active role in the development of industries. The 1948 resolution specified that arms and ammunition, atomic energy and railway transport would be exclusively under the central government; as would be new undertakings in six basic industries except where, in the national interest, the state considered it necessary to secure the cooperation of private enterprise. Other industries were to be open to the private sector, though the resolution was clear that the state would also progressively participate in these industries.

This was followed by large-scale industrial licencing under the Industries (Development and Regulation) Act, 1951 (IDRA). Section 11 of the IDRA stated, 'No person or authority other than the Central Government shall . . . establish any new industrial undertaking, except under and in accordance with a licence issued in that behalf by the Central Government.' The First Schedule of the Act contained a mammoth list of industrial activities that needed licencing.[122] Overnight almost, an enterprise

[122] Licences were needed for production of metals, minerals, fuels, boilers, prime movers, electrical, telecommunications and transportation equipment, fertilizers, sugar, industrial machinery, machine tools, vegetable oils, drugs and

needed an industrial licence to establish a new undertaking, manufacture a new product in an existing undertaking, expand capacities, change location, and much more. Over the years, the list continued expanding to Orwellian proportions, with the procedures for obtaining a licence becoming even more elaborate and bizarre.

Then came the Industrial Policy Resolution (IPR) on 30 April 1956 and, with it, product reservation for the public sector. The IPR made 'adoption of the socialist pattern of society as the national objective', and this was sought to be achieved through expansion of the public sector via reservations. It defined three types of industries:

• Seventeen Schedule A industries 'of basic and strategic importance, or in the nature of public utilities' whose development was to be 'the exclusive responsibility of the state';[123]

---

pharmaceuticals, paints and dyes, rubber goods, ceramics and hundreds of other items including profoundly critical ones such as linoleum, pressure cookers, cutlery, hurricane lanterns and, believe it or not, zip fasteners!

[123] These were: (i) arms, ammunition and defence equipment; (ii) atomic energy; (iii) iron and steel; (iv) heavy castings and forgings of iron and steel; (v) heavy plant and machinery required for iron and steel production, for mining, for machine tool manufacture and for such other basic industries as specified by the central government; (vi) heavy electrical plant including large hydraulic and steam turbines; (vii) coal and lignite; (viii) mineral oils; (ix) mining of iron ore, manganese ore, chrome ore, gypsum, sulphur, gold and diamond; (x) mining and processing of copper, lead, zinc, tin, molybdenum

- Twelve Schedule B industries where the state was expected to 'increasingly establish new undertaking'; and
- The residual industries, which would typically be in the domain of the private sector 'though it will be open to the state to start any industry even in this category'.

In 1955, two other developments occurred, which, coupled with Nehru's socialist rhetoric, struck fear in the hearts of entrepreneurs. One involved the nationalization of all private sector insurance businesses, which affected British and Indian managing agencies alike; and the other was the central government taking over the great colonial financial institution, the Imperial Bank of India, and rechristening it as the State Bank of India (SBI).[124]

The IPR coincided with the Second Five Year Plan (1956–61). Based on a 1928 Soviet planning model and formulated by Nehru's favourite economic adviser P.C. Mahalanobis of the Indian Statistical Institute, the Second

---

and wolfram; (xi) minerals specified in the Schedule to the Atomic Energy (Control of Production and Use) Order, 1953; (xii) aircraft; (xiii) air transport; (xiv) railway transport; (xv) ship building; (xvi) telephones, telephone cables, telegraph and wireless apparatus excluding radio receiving sets; and (xvii) generation and distribution of electricity.

[124] In 1959, the government passed the State Bank of India (Subsidiary Banks) Act which nationalized eight SBI subsidiaries located in the former princely states such as in Travancore and Hyderabad. Operationally taken over during 1959–60, these became subsidiaries and associates of the SBI.

Plan proposed rapid economic growth through major investments in heavy industries. In its own words:

> 'The Second Five Year plan accords high priority to industrialisation, and especially to the development of basic and heavy industries. A large expansion of public enterprise in the sphere of industrial and mineral development is envisaged. It is, in fact, intended to strengthen further the programmes of development in respect of heavy industries, oil exploration and coal and to make a beginning with the development of atomic energy. The main responsibility for these programmes rests upon the Central Government.'[125]

When the Second Plan document was being discussed, it came under serious criticism from private business. G.D. Birla, who considered the plan impractical, led a delegation to meet Nehru in January 1956 to register a strong protest. In the meantime, his magazine, *The Eastern Economist*, called Mahalanobis 'a statistician completely devoid of a sense of economic organisation' and berated him for creating a 'theoretical shibboleth which, if enforced, would in one sweep endanger India's future industrialisation'.[126] At Rs 4,800 crore (Rs 48,000 million), the size of the plan was held by the delegation to

[125] Government of India, *The Second Five Year Plan (1956–61)*, Chapter 2, paragraph 12.
[126] Kudaisya (2003), p. 315.

be wholly impractical and 'utterly beyond the resources of the country'—one that could be met only by incurring huge fiscal deficits, consequent inflation and draining of India's scarce foreign currency reserves.

All this was to no avail. Though its size was marginally curtailed, the Second Plan came into being with its public sector-based heavy industrialization approach remaining intact. For all its subsequent drawbacks, there is no doubt that the plan created the foundation for large-scale industrial growth which, in truth, was well beyond the ken of most Indian and all British managing agencies.

Four huge integrated steel plants came into being under state ownership: Bhilai with Soviet assistance in 1959; Durgapur with help from the UK in 1959–60; Rourkela under German supervision in 1960; and Bokaro, also with Soviet knowhow in 1964. The Heavy Engineering Corporation was set up in Ranchi in 1958. The National Mineral Development Corporation opened for business in the same year. The Fertilizer Corporation of India came into being in 1961 when the central government consolidated five state-run plants under a single public sector entity. Bharat Heavy Electricals Limited was established in 1964. And in 1953, with the nationalization of air transportation under the Air Corporations Act, Air India, the 1946-avatar of Tata Airlines and the object of J.R.D. Tata's loving care, passed on to the government of India. As did Hindustan Aircraft, started by Walchand Hirachand, which became Hindustan Aeronautics Limited in 1964.

Then there were the dams that Nehru called 'temples of modern India'. The Bhakra Nangal project, comprising two dams, came up on the Sutlej to irrigate eastern Punjab; the Damodar Valley Corporation built the Maithon, Panchet and Tilaiya dams in what is now Jharkhand; the Tungabhadra dam at Hospet was greatly expanded; the Hirakud dam on the Mahanadi was completed in 1953 and inaugurated by Nehru in 1957; the Koyna dam, which was strong enough to withstand a major earthquake in 1967, was built between 1956 and 1964 in the district of Satara in Maharashtra; the Kota Barrage and the Rana Pratap Sagar dams were built in Rajasthan; and more were in the offing.

Indian Businesses Still Grew

It would be all too facile and factually incorrect to claim that the growth of large state-owned enterprises and the creation of dams and public irrigation under Nehru, Lal Bahadur Shastri and even in the early years of Indira Gandhi created an economic environment that sucked up scarce fiscal and financial resources and thus 'crowded out' private sector investments. From the late 1950s right up to the early 1970s, public sector investment created an environment of 'crowding in' by encouraging a wide array of related ancillary activities that were provided by private industry. As an example, the Bhakra dam, whose construction started in 1948 at Bilaspur in what is today's Himachal Pradesh, led to a huge demand for cement that was supplied by ACC, Rohtas Industries and several other privately run cement manufacturers of north and central India. It also led to engineering and construction contracts that benefited many new firms, of which Escorts, the post-partition Delhi-based company started by H.P. Nanda and his brother Yudhisthir, was one. The same was the story with other dams that came up in that era.

Likewise, the steel plants not only led to the building of large manufacturing complexes and townships that were a boon for civil, mechanical and electrical contractors, but also created an environment for several associated industries. After the setting up of the Durgapur steel plant, there followed many privately owned businesses such as ACC-Vickers Babcock for making boilers, Philips Carbon Black, Sankey Wheels of Guest, Keen Williams, Graphite India, Durgapur Chemicals and Ispat Forging, not to mention scores of mid-sized forging and steel bar drawing companies that transformed semi-finished steel ingots from the huge state-owned plant into various types of intermediate and finished products.[127]

[127] Though Nehru clearly favoured public sector led industrialization and didn't much care for some of the Marwari businessmen that he had to meet, he was clearly not against private industry. In a speech to the Parliament, he said, 'I have no shadow of doubt that if we say 'lop off the private sector', we cannot replace it. We haven't got the resources to replace it, and the result would be that our productive apparatus would suffer. And why should we do it, I do not understand. Let the state go on building up its plants and its industries as far as its resources permit. Why should we fritter away our energy in pushing out somebody who is doing it in the private sector?. . . [Where] there is such a vast field to cover, it is foolish to take charge

It is not surprising, therefore, that despite the so-called reservations for the public sector under the IPR 1956, the Nehruvian era witnessed fairly rapid growth of private industry under the aegis of Indian managing agencies and the new MNCs. The largest Indian group was the Tatas, with J.R.D. Tata at the helm in Bombay House. Suave, polite and anglicized enough to meet the approval of Nehru, his key cabinet ministers and the many secretaries of the Government of India, J.R.D. succeeded in getting the necessary permits, licensing and funding from within India and the World Bank to double TISCO's steel-making capacity from 1 million to 2 million metric tons by 1958. Steel may have been exclusively reserved for the public sector under Schedule A of the IPR 1956, but TISCO was special. So too was the group's New India Assurance Company which, despite nationalization of insurance, continued undisturbed as a private sector entity until it was taken over by the central government in 1973.

The Tata Locomotive and Engineering Company was reorganized to become the Tata Engineering and Locomotive Company (TELCO) which, along with Tata Chemicals, Tata Oil Mills and Tata Power, were under the control of Tata Industries, one of the two major managing agencies of the group. Originally, TELCO made locomotives for a single customer, the Indian Railways.

---

of the whole field when you are totally incapable of using that huge area yourself.' Quoted in Tripathi and Jumani (2007), pp. 150–51.

In 1954, it diversified into the manufacture of trucks in collaboration with Daimler-Benz of Germany. It started with production of 3,000 vehicles in 1955; doubled it in the next three years; doubled that yet again, and again; and by the late 1960s, its trucks, along with those of Leyland, which was founded in Ennore, north of Madras, by Raghunandan Saran in 1948, became ubiquitous on Indian highways. TELCO's collaboration with Daimler-Benz ended in 1969, but it continued to operate at full capacity afterwards. Tata Chemicals and Tata Oil Mills also grew throughout the period, although the former was denied a licence to diversify into fertilizers in 1967— which it eventually did much later.

The Tatas also made new acquisitions. One was the Bombay-based British managing agency of Forbes Forbes, Campbell & Company along with its various industrial interests. It also took over a Swiss trading company called Volkart Brothers in 1954, rechristened it Voltas Limited and focused on the production and trade of air conditioning equipment as well as agricultural and industrial machinery. In 1963, it went into a partnership with James Finlay, another British managing agency based in both Calcutta and Bombay, with interests in tea. The new company was called Tata Finlay, which later became Tata Tea.

The biggest loss for the Tata group, and personally for J.R.D., was Air India International. Launched in 1948 as a joint venture, with the Tatas holding 20 per cent equity, the Government of India 49 per cent and the investing public 31 per cent, it was J.R.D.'s baby. By 1956, following the IPR, it was nationalized. J.R.D. protested as best as he could. But his complaints came to naught. Other than making him the titular chairman of Air India, a role that J.R.D. took more seriously than any of his successors, the enterprise became yet another public sector entity. But with a difference. Thanks to J.R.D.'s indefatigable zeal and eye for quality, and Bobby Kooka's masterly use of the stylized Maharaja in selling the airline, Air India remained a top class brand till Tata put in his papers—after which it was run by successive ministers and civil servants, and kept going downhill to the pathetic state that it is in today.

For all the constraints it faced—being refused expansion licences for Tata Chemicals, Tata Electric, TELCO and TISCO (beyond doubling of capacity in 1958) and the loss of Air India—the Tata group retained its preeminent position among all Indian-controlled businesses and grew revenues at roughly 6 per cent per year, from Rs 163 crore (Rs 1,630 million) in 1950–51 to more than Rs 500 crore (Rs 5,000 million) in 1969. Many acquisitions helped it increase its span of control, from 102 companies to over 150 over the same period.

The group that grew the fastest were the Birlas, through the setting up of new, large-scale ventures and relentless acquisitions, all of which were organized across three managing agencies, Birla Brothers, Birla Gwalior and, to a lesser extent, Hindustan Investment Corporation. Among their acquisitions were Century Spinning and Weaving Mills, a Bombay mill originally set up by the Wadias and later came under the control of Chunilal Mehta; Digvijay Cotton in Saurashtra; Bally,

Rameshwar and Soorah jute mill companies in and around Calcutta; Sirpur and Orient paper mills; the Sirsilk mill; Hyderabad Asbestos and Air Conditioning Corporation.

There were various diversifications as well, for which the Birlas almost always seemed to get the licences. Kesoram ventured into production of rayon; Jiyajeerao Cotton Mills in Gwalior started manufacturing chemicals; Birla Jute widened its net to accommodate cement and chemicals. G.D. also set up new companies such as Digvijay Woollen Mills and Gwalior Rayon, located in Nagda (Central Provinces, now Madhya Pradesh), which became the first rayon producer in India; Hindustan Motors in Uttarpara, West Bengal which, in alliance with Morris of Oxford, began producing first Morris Minors and then the Morris Oxford, better known as India's omnipresent Ambassador; TEXMACO, which started production of textile machinery and then went on to manufacture railway wagons; and Zuari Agro Chemicals in Goa to manufacture fertilizers.

But by far the biggest investment of the Birla group during the period was Hindustan Aluminium Company Limited (HINDALCO). G.D. planned the project in great detail with his favourite son Basant Kumar (B.K.), going to the US in 1957 to meet Edgar Kaiser, the industrialist who headed a huge conglomerate called Kaiser Corporation that specialized in the manufacture of non-ferrous metals. An agreement was inked in 1957–58 for a 20,000 metric ton plant at a capital cost of Rs 15 crore (Rs 150 million)—a huge sum at the time. After securing long-term credit at advantageous terms from the

Export-Import Bank of the US, the equity component
was split, with Kaiser Corporation holding 26 per cent,
Birla Gwalior owning 25 per cent and the public 49 per
cent. Chitra Bhanu Gupta, the most prominent politician
from the United Provinces (later Uttar Pradesh) and
soon to be the fourth chief minister of the state, prevailed
upon G.D. to set up the plant near the Rihand dam. G.D.
acquiesced, and after finalizing advantageous long-term
power tariffs as well as major bauxite mining leases, set
up the HINDALCO plant in a record time of eighteen
months in Renukoot. Commercial production at the
plant began in October 1962. The next expansion of
capacity to 40,000 tons, followed by another of 20,000
tons, required building a captive power plant, which too
Birla did.[128]

For all his successes in the new licence-control raj,
even G.D. had his setbacks. He was very keen on setting
up a full-fledged steel mill, which Bidhan Chandra Roy,
the chief minister of West Bengal, suggested that he
locate in Durgapur. The industry minister of the time,
Harekrushna Mahatab, and Nehru's finance minister,
T.T. Krishnamachari, were optimistic that the licence
would be granted. But it was not to be. Birla's proposal
to set up a plant producing 250,000 tons of pig iron and 1
million tons of steel was turned down by a committee led
by Nehru. The other disappointment was Bharat Airways
set up by B.K., which was nationalized in 1953.[129]

[128] Kudaisya (2003), pp. 334–35.
[129] *Ibid.*, pp. 333–34.

Still, the Birlas advanced rapidly. To be sure, the group could not overtake the Tatas to be numero uno in independent India. But it grew at a faster rate than the Tatas and, by the end of the 1960s, was clearly number two. Together, the two giants controlled a fifth of the assets of the private corporate sector.[130]

Despite licencing and controls, other Indian groups too were enjoying the fruits of freedom. The family of Mafatlal Gagalbhai, having made large profits in textiles, bought two other large mill companies, one in Bombay and the other in Dewas. In 1954, it then acquired Indian Dyestuffs Industries at Kalyan near Bombay, and diversified into petrochemicals by setting up two major manufacturing companies: National Organic Chemical Industries with American knowhow, and Polyolefins Industries Limited with German collaboration. Both were large in size, and propelled the group to third position in the corporate pecking order.[131]

Karam Chand Thapar continued to grow in size and scale. From his ventures in coal, sugar and insurance based out of east India, Thapar forayed into textiles, setting up the Jagatjit Cotton Textile Mills at Phagwara in Punjab. He then acquired Greaves Cotton followed by its affiliate Crompton Greaves, which were involved in engineering products, motors and electrical equipment. Already in paper with Shree Gopal Paper Mills, Thapar then bought out Ballarpur Paper and Straw Board Mills,

[130] Ibid., p. 336.
[131] Tripathi and Jumani (2007), pp. 162–63.

and then merged the two in 1969 to create a significant paper conglomerate. Spanning coal, sugar, cotton textiles, engineering and paper, Karam Chand Thapar & Brothers became the fourth largest business entity in the country by the late 1960s.[132]

The Kirloskars, of whom the suited, bow-tied MIT graduate Shantanu L. Kirloskar was the most prominent face, continued to focus on and grow their businesses of engines and agricultural equipment with Kirloskar Oil, Kirloskar Pneumatic, Kirloskar Electric and Kirloskar Cummins. Given his hatred for the corridors of power and his penchant for blunt speech, Shantanu Kirloskar remained a Poona man, more at home growing his group's businesses and understanding new technologies and modes of management than hobnobbing in New Delhi, which had become the norm for Indian entrepreneurs.

The Mahindras were of a similar vein. Set up as a steel trading company in 1945 in Ludhiana as Mahindra & Mohammed by two brothers, K.C. and J.C. Mahindra, and Malik Ghulam Mohammed, it changed its name to Mahindra & Mahindra in 1948 after Mohammed left for Pakistan. Having moved to Bombay, it graduated from distribution of Willy's Jeeps in India to licenced manufacture. Through various technical collaborations, long-term loans and foreign equity participation, the next generation of Keshub and Harish Mahindra went into manufacture of tractors, alloy steel and hydraulic

[132] *Ibid.*, p. 162.

equipment. Like the Kirloskars, the group was known for its business honesty and probity.[133]

Jamnalal Bajaj died in 1942. After him, the business passed on to his elder son, Kamalnayan. Though the sugar mills, ginning and trading businesses were doing reasonably well, the group was struggling with Mukand Iron and Steel Works, which it had acquired in 1939, and which had one unit in Bombay and the other in Lahore. Before things could be turned around, Partition saw the end of the Lahore operations. Slowly, however, the group began to grow its businesses through careful acquisition of factories that produced bulbs, lamps, tube lights and fans in Bombay and Uttar Pradesh between 1954 and 1958, which were later to form the core of Bajaj Electricals. In 1961, a collaboration with Piaggio led to manufacture of the Vespa and three-wheelers at Bajaj Auto Limited's new factory in Akurdi near Poona.[134] By 1970, Bajaj Auto, then under Kamalnayan's son Rahul, had produced 100,000 scooters; it was a brand so popular that one could sell the allotment note for the vehicle in a trice at double the price. With this company, the Bajaj group had arrived.[135]

The Godrej group, founded by Ardeshir and Pirojsha Godrej in 1897, progressed at a more stately pace. Before

---

[133] *Ibid.*, pp. 163–64 and pp. 167–68.

[134] In addition to the existing paid-up capital of Rs 9.9 lakh, an IPO of Rs 60.1 lakh comprising 60,100 shares of Rs 100 each (25,740 shares for existing equity owners and 34,360 shares for the public) was oversubscribed in 1961.

[135] Gita Piramal, *Kamalnayan Bajaj: Architect of the Bajaj Group*, Kamalnayan Bajaj Charitable Trust, 2015.

Independence, it had a modest presence in products like safes, locks, refined oils and toilet soap. After 1947, it expanded to make typewriters and office equipment, followed by refrigerators in the 1960s. Unlike most Indian entrepreneurs, the Godrej family did not believe in listing their companies and ran all their businesses through two closely held private firms, Godrej & Boyce and Godrej Soaps. Notwithstanding their innate conservatism, the various businesses expanded considerably between 1947 and 1970.

Then there were the industrialists who came from nowhere after Independence to create large businesses within a few decades. With Partition, Escorts, under H.P. Nanda, lost its agency to distribute Westinghouse products, and moved from Lahore to Delhi, rebuilding itself with a transport business and buying, renovating and reselling second-hand cars that were sold en masse by the British leaving for home. It soon got into general contracting, made a fortune during the building of the Bhakra and Nangal dams, and then moved into manufacturing—first pistons, followed by Ford tractors, earth movers and then motorcycles, all under collaborative agreements. By 1970, Escorts had become one of the twenty-five top listed companies in India.

No less determined was the effort of Brij Mohan Lall Munjal, who escaped from Pakistan to set up a small cycle repair shop in Ludhiana that steadily grew to become Hero Cycles—which then overtook two others, Avon and Atlas, also set up by refugees, to become the largest cycle manufacturer in the world. Similarly, Vittal

Mallya, who started as a stockbroker in Calcutta, steadily built up positions in a Bangalore-based British firm called United Breweries, then acquired a controlling interest in it, culminating in his family taking over the firm shortly after 1947.[136]

That brings us to the four major acquirers among the Marwaris of Calcutta: the Bajorias, the Bangurs, the Khaitans and the Goenkas. Like most Marwari banias associated with the jute trade and the mill industry, the Bajorias used their trading profits to steadily build considerable equity stakes in various companies run by British managing agencies. By the 1960s, the family took control of most of the jute mills and tea plantations run by McLeod & Company. The Bangurs, also significant shareholders in many expatriate-controlled jute mill companies prior to 1947, made their acquisition plays after Independence. By the mid-1950s, in addition to controlling a sugar mill, they had taken over the managing agency of Kettlewell Bullen & Company, which controlled a pair each of jute and cotton mill companies. In the 1960s, the Bangurs took over Bengal Coal and Midnapore Zemindary from Andrew Yule & Company.[137]

The other significant acquirer was Brij Mohan (B.M.) Khaitan, whose shrewdly created empire was dormant before Independence, sticking as he did to supplying fertilizers and packing crates to many tea plantations

---

[136] Tripathi and Jumani (2007), pp. 174–75 and *IIYB, 1961*, p. 261 and p. 391.

[137] *IIYB 1962*, sections on sugar, jute, cotton and miscellaneous industries.

in Assam. That got him very close to Richard Magor, the managing partner of Williamson Magor, a British managing agency that had shrunk in size from being the largest in tea to one that controlled ten listed companies. Fearing a takeover from less sophisticated Marwaris, Magor offered B.M. a third of the shares in the firm. Soon enough, and with all his charm at his disposal, B.M. bought out the remaining shares of Williamson Magor to become the largest tea garden owner in the world.[138]

The most spectacular ascent through acquisitions was that of the Goenkas. The patriarch, Sir Badridas, remained content as one of Calcutta's biggest banias, a large shareholder in many jute mills, corporate moneylender to British managing agencies in their times of need and director on the boards of several expatriate companies. Not so his eldest son Keshav Prasad (K.P.). During the 1950s, in carefully calibrated stages, he took control of the Anglo-India Jute Mill Company, hitherto managed by Duncan Brothers, in addition to taking over Hukumchand Jute. He then took over some companies under Octavius Steel. Soon he was training his sights on all companies under the management of Duncan. These included eighteen listed tea gardens, Philips Carbon Black, and other miscellaneous enterprises. This was followed up by the acquisition of Asian Cables in Bombay, which gave K.P. a bridgehead in India's most dynamic business metropolis. There was no looking back after that. The family of Sir Badridas Goenka, which began business as

---

[138] Tripathi and Jumani (2007), pp. 170–71.

a nineteenth century jute trading firm called Ramdutt Ramkissendas, had arrived on the industrial stage.

South India, dormant in industrial entrepreneurship during the colonial era, suddenly picked up pace. At the time of Independence, there were only a few firms controlled by T.V. Sundaram Iyengar & Sons. With tough import restrictions coming into play in the 1960s, the group saw the potential of rapid growth through import substitution. That saw the setting up of a slew of auto component ventures such as Wheels India, Lucas-TVS, Sundaram-Clayton, Brakes India, Sundram Fasteners and some others—most of which were developed through foreign equity or through technical collaborations.[139]

Amalgamations Limited, a British firm that had passed on to S. Anantharamakrishnan (strangely called 'J') got into the manufacture of automotive paints through Addison Paints, pistons (India Pistons) and automobile batteries (Amco Batteries). J then set up Tractors and Farm Equipment (TAFE) in collaboration with Massey Ferguson of the UK to produce tractors. TAFE is a company now managed by J's granddaughter Mallika Srinivasan. Soon the group controlled over forty companies ranging from bookstores, such as Madras's famous Higginbothams, and plantations to tractors and auto components. The family of Sankaralinga Iyer and his son K.S. Narayan founded India Cements in 1946 and Chemplast Sanmar in 1962; the former is now under

---

[139] Harish Damodaran, *India's New Capitalists: Caste, Business and Industry in a Modern Nation*, Permanent Black, 2008, pp. 57–8.

N. Srinivasan, he of the Board of Cricket Control of India fame (or infamy), while the latter is run by N. Sankar and N. Kumar.[140]

The A.M. Murugappa Chettiar group, after suffering huge losses in moneylending and rice trading in Burma in the 1930s and relocating to Madras, moved into industry only after 1947—starting with the Coromandel Engineering Company in 1947, then T.I. Cycles in 1949, followed by Carborandum Universal in 1954, Tubes Product of India in 1955, and several other metal tubes and abrasives manufacturing ventures, finally capping it all with the acquisition of E.I.D. Parry.[141] The family of Raja Sir Annamalai Chettiar and his son Sir M.A. Muthiah Chettiar also got into industries after independence, as did the Kamma and Kongunnad Naidus around Madras, Andhra Pradesh and Coimbatore. Late to start, south India got going by the 1960s.

Thus, despite the socialist rhetoric, licences, control, central planning and the growing presence of large state-owned enterprises under Jawaharlal Nehru, India saw a fairly impressive growth of private sector enterprise. With it grew the economy too. GDP at factor cost and constant prices increased at an average annual rate of 3.7 per cent for the period 1950–51 to 1970–71. No doubt the public sector grew at a more rapid rate. However, even in 1970–71, six years after Nehru's death, it accounted for

[140] *Ibid.*, pp. 58–60.
[141] From http://en.wikipedia.org/wiki/Murugappa_Group; and the group company details in the Murugappa website.

no more than 14 per cent of GDP—and that included all the apparatus of government, not just state-owned enterprises. This was scarcely a story of unbridled state domination of manufacturing, as feared with the IPR of 1956.

There is also no doubt that the industrial sector did well over these two decades. It clearly shows up in the national income data. At a time when GDP increased at an average of 3.7 per cent per year, both manufacturing and the secondary sector grew significantly faster—with the former steadily increasing its share in GDP from 9 per cent in 1950–51 to 12.7 per cent in 1970–71, and the latter from 16.2 per cent to 23.6 per cent. This was driven by Indian industry, be it the public sector or companies controlled by Indian entrepreneurial groups.

The MNCs

By the mid-1930s, and more so in the 1940s and 1950s, another breed of corporate player entered India: the large multinational company headquartered in Britain, the US or continental Europe. Consider Unilever, the Anglo-Dutch consumer foods giant that came into being in 1929. In 1933, within four years of its global incorporation, it began operations in India out of Bombay as a private limited company called Lever Brothers (India) Limited. In another five years, and using its own marketing, advertising and distribution network, Lever Brothers became so successful in selling Sunlight and Lifebuoy soaps that the president of the Indian Soap

Manufacturers Association publicly complained of unfair competition backed by huge capital outlays driving out the smaller, patriotic Indian soap makers.[142] In October 1956, the company went public and renamed itself Hindustan Lever Limited. By 1961, with paid-up capital of Rs 5.6 crore and led by the legendary Prakash Lal (P.L.) Tandon, Hindustan Lever was everywhere—selling Sunlight, Lifebuoy, Lux, Rexona and Pears soaps, Vim scouring powder, Dalda *vanaspati*, Pepsodent and Gibbs toothpastes, Surf detergent powder, Erasmic shaving stick and much more. Growing in leaps and bounds, its net profit for 1961 was Rs 2.5 crore, higher than what many other companies, whether managed by British or Indian managing agencies, were reporting.[143]

Lever was but one such MNC. In lighting and electrical products, India saw entry of the British arm of General Electric Company and the Dutch MNC Philips of Eindhoven. With the spread of electrification and the use of radios, Philips was reaping an EBITDA (earnings before interest, taxes, depreciation and amortization) of Rs 49 lakh in 1960, and getting ready for some major capacity expansion. Brooke Bond and Lipton from the UK entered in the inter-war years and introduced the revolutionary concept of packaged, blended and standardized tea. Dunlop was in India since 1926. By 1961, with factories outside Calcutta and Madras manufacturing tyres and

[142] Speech of Mari Shankar Paul, Indian Soap Manufacturers Association, *Hindustan Standard*, 1 January 1938.
[143] *IIYB 1961*, p. 331.

rubber goods and with paid-up capital of Rs 5.2 crore, its EBITDA amounted to Rs 2.3 crore. Goodyear of Akron, Ohio, was a US entrant that started business in the subcontinent by exporting tyres and then moved on to manufacturing. In India from 1910, Imperial Tobacco graduated from being a private company to a publicly listed one in 1954. Headquartered in the imposing Virginia House on Chowringhee, Calcutta, its cigarettes sold everywhere. In 1961, with paid-up capital of Rs 15.2 crore, it reported an EBITDA of Rs 2.3 crore.[144]

MNCs, listed or otherwise, entered every sector that promised growth. Imperial Chemical Industries set up ICI (India) Limited under which it promoted the Alkali and Chemical Corporation of India to manufacture industrial chemicals from its factory at Rishra, near Calcutta. By 1961, the company had posted an EBITDA of Rs 1.3 crore on paid-up capital of Rs 3.4 crore.[145] Global oil majors such as Burmah Shell, Caltex and Stan-Vac (as Esso) soon controlled and cartelized the entire petroleum, kerosene, aviation fuel and lube oil network.[146] Guest, Keen, Nettlefolds, an engineering major of the UK, started Guest, Keen, Williams in India to manufacture

[144] *Ibid.*, section on miscellaneous companies.
[145] *Ibid.*, p. 286.
[146] They also hired well at salaries significantly greater than what was paid by most British and Indian managing agencies. My father, after graduating from the Bengal Engineering College (Sibpur) in 1948, was recruited by Caltex for a princely salary of Rs 700 per month and a shiny Dodge De Soto to boot. He stayed there till just before nationalization in 1970.

specialized railway equipment in Howrah and Bhandup, near Bombay. With paid-up capital of Rs 4 crore in 1961, it posted an EBITDA of Rs 1.2 crore.[147] Babcock & Wilcox began a wholly owned subsidiary to manufacture large-scale boilers for India's new manufacturing plants. Metal Box of the UK incorporated Metal Box Company (India) Limited, which went public in 1949. Manufacturing metal containers, closures, stamping machines and bottle tops, it was another profitable MNC operation, with its EBITDA at Rs 80 lakh against its paid-up capital of Rs 1.9 crore.[148] Jenson & Nicholson manufactured paints, enamels, varnish and distemper, as did Goodlass Wall, which became Goodlass Nerolac and went public in 1957. British Oxygen entered and founded Indian Oxygen to supply industrial gas; Colgate-Palmolive came in to compete with Hindustan Lever to sell toothpaste in urban India; Chloride joined the fray to manufacture batteries, as did Union Carbide, which set up Union Carbide (India) Limited that reported an EBITDA of over Rs 1 crore on paid-up capital of Rs 2.8 crore; and Alcan of Canada started the Indian Aluminium Company which, by 1961, was earning post-depreciation profit of Rs 1.7 crore on paid-up capital of Rs 4.4 crore.[149]

Most of the MNCs grew rapidly and earned profits much higher than the typical jute and cotton mills, collieries, tea gardens, engineering companies and

[147] *IIYB 1961*, p. 262.
[148] *Ibid.*, pp. 357–58.
[149] *Ibid.*, pp. 338–39 and p. 391.

miscellaneous enterprises controlled by British and Indian managing agencies did. That was but natural: these global (India) limited companies were in a different league altogether in terms of scale, scope, size and management. Their growth had much to do with the changing patterns of consumer and industrial demand, thanks to the relatively rapid industrialization that occurred after the mid-1950s. The population in the cities had increased significantly and, by the early 1960s, there were many in urban India that preferred packaged to loose tea, cigarettes to bidis, toothpaste to rough dental powder and neem sticks, decent soap, and affordable hydrogenated vegetable oil such as Dalda. Industrial growth led to the demand for non-ferrous extrusions, engineering products, industrial gases, batteries, paint, boilers, motors, automobile and truck tyres and more—all of which was being supplied in the required scale and quality by the MNCs. It is not surprising, therefore, that by the late 1960s, profits of British MNCs in India were 120 per cent of their world average. It was a great country to be in.[150]

An interesting feature of such (India) Limited companies was that they had little or no commercial truck with the British managing agencies. It was not for want of trying by the latter, who were only too keen to tie up with the British MNCs when they entered the country. Their pitch was that, having been in the heat and dust of India for decades on end, they knew all the intricacies of the subcontinent's markets. Indeed there were some early

[150] B.R. Tomlinson, 'British Firms in India', mimeo, 1982.

tie-ups before World War II. Unfortunately, the British managing agencies proved to be woefully inept and, by the early 1950s, the MNCs decided to operate without any help from the raj-era boxwallahs. If anything, the MNCs tended to interact and cooperate with each other. ICI (India) helped Metal Box in its initial marketing; Metal Box supplied containers to Caltex, Burmah Shell and Esso, placing its own roofing orders with another MNC Asbestos Cement. Besides cooperating with one another, these MNCs created their own marketing and distribution channels, often taking their cues from how the parent companies did business in similar countries.

Exit of British Managing Agencies

As indicated earlier, little had changed in the structure of ownership and corporate control between a decade before Independence and the mid-1950s. Despite the rapid growth of Indian, especially Marwari, control over jute mills and collieries, both industries continued to be dominated by British managing agencies. In tea, the British presence was stronger still. The changes started from 1956, especially after the coming of public sector reservations under the IPR. And, despite the terms 'managing agency' and 'secretary' being retained in the new Companies Act of 1956, and despite assurances from the government that British corporate interests would be protected, the law actually imposed serious restrictions on various commission- and profit-earning activities of managing agencies.

The environment—legal, political, economic and business—was becoming hostile for the British managing agencies. Increasingly cornered, many of these firms started to get an idea of the shape of things to come. In Calcutta, one Marwari business house or the other, armed with sufficient shares of some of the listed companies under British control, were snapping at their heels and waiting for the earliest chance of a takeover. Besides, the post-Independence era had become entrepreneurially more competitive, and required faster, nimbler decision-making. In truth, only a few colonials could consistently demonstrate strategic capabilities, speed and imaginative execution—coming as most of them did as second, third or poor cousins of the Scottish and English partners to oversee modest manufacturing and unsophisticated mining in an environment where their lot ruled the nation. Largely ill-educated, untrained and unimaginative chaps, these colonial managers were least prepared for the changes that occurred with industrial licencing and public sector reservations, and the simple fact that the central and state governments were now being run by yesterday's adversaries. Besides, they knew little or nothing of the new industries and businesses that were defining a fast industrializing, independent nation. A tired lot after enjoying the good times for over seventy-five years, they were ready to pack their bags and go home.

It was also becoming clear to them that the business capital of independent India was Bombay, not Calcutta. Once called 'Paris of the East', the metropolis on the

banks of the Hooghly had become very difficult to carry
on work in. Refugees from East Pakistan had swamped
the city; jute mills were now centres of serious labour
agitations; yesterday's pliant Bengali clerks and babus
were now often seen spouting their rights; the wealthier
Marwaris had constructed enormous homes in hitherto
pristinely white enclaves like Alipore and Belvedere;
and Trincas, Firpo, Skyroom, the Tolly, Royal Calcutta,
Calcutta Cricket and Football Club, the Bengal Club and
the city's once famous new year's eve parties, while still
popular, were not enough to keep the sahibs and their
mems in the heat and sweat of the city. It is not surprising
that the major change in corporate control from British
to Indian managing agencies occurred by 1961, as seen
in Table 8.

Table 8: How British managing agencies shrank

Industry	1950–51			1961		
	No. of cos.	British MAs	Indian MAs	No. of cos.	British MAs	Indian MAs
Coal	48	55%	43%	42	43%	57%
Cotton	62	31%	69%	60	12%	88%
Tea	124	91%	9%	127	40%	60%
Jute	59	80%	18%	55	40%	58%
Sugar	25	48%	52%	26	12%	88%
Engineering	25	64%	36%	32	12%	88%
Miscellaneous	123	55%	42%	169	36%	59%
Total	**483**	**64%**	**35%**	**511**	**32%**	**66%**

Source: IIYB, 1952 and 1961.

As the table shows, from controlling 80 per cent of the listed jute mill companies in 1950–51, the British managing agencies saw their corporate writ reduce to 40 per cent in 1961. In coal, their control dropped from 55 per cent of the companies to 43 per cent; and in tea, the changes were more precipitous, their control over 91 per cent of listed tea gardens in 1950–51 dipping to 40 per cent in 1961. Signs of their retreat were everywhere: they were down from controlling 31 per cent of the cotton textile mills to 12 per cent; from 48 per cent of listed sugar mills to 12 per cent; from 64 per cent of engineering companies to 12 per cent; and from 55 per cent of other miscellaneous companies to 36 per cent.

Some expatriate managing agencies such as Begg Sutherland of Kanpur and Kettlewell Bullen were ready to sell their interest at any price to quickly repatriate what they could and return home. Thomas Duff & Company, which managed three jute mills and an engineering works, sold to Girdharilal Mehta for £700,000.[151] Mehta also bought the commanding interests of Jardine Skinner. McLeod and Duncan Brothers attempted a more orderly exit by gradually selling companies under their control, the former largely to the Bajoria and Jalan families, and the latter to K.P. Goenka. Andrew Yule also sold its interests in various collieries, jute mills and tea plantations in bits and pieces to various Marwari groups of Calcutta; their residual interests were finally nationalized by the central

---

[151] Misra (1999), p. 193.

government in the late 1960s. Some collapsed under the
weight of mismanagement and labour unrest—the most
notable being Martin Burn, by now under the control of
Sir Biren Mukherjee. It was finally nationalized in 1972,
along with its flagship Indian Iron and Steel Company
(IISCO).[152]

Bird & Company and its affiliate F.W. Heilgers were
in a slightly different position. While both divested some
of their holdings to Marwari banias long associated with
their managing agencies, the group, then under the
leadership of A.P. (Paul) Benthall, the younger brother
of Sir Edward, was determined to remain in the county
of its choice. Unfortunately, in 1964, Bird was badly hit
by a large demand for unpaid customs duty and Benthall
decided enough was enough. The exit, however, took
a different route. Instead of selling out the residual
companies to Indian managing agencies eagerly waiting
to pounce, Paul Benthall allowed the group's senior
Indian management and employees to buy out the
British controlling interests through their provident and
pension funds. Sadly for the firm and the companies that
it managed, most of the new owners were incompetent
and some corrupt, and the businesses failed year after
year from the late 1960s. Eventually, the group was taken

---

[152] Sir Biren Mookerjee, son of the founder of IISCO, Sir Rajendra
Nath, who ran the group as well as IISCO, said, 'I see before
my eyes a vast industrial complex with which I was associated
for some 40 years crumbling to dust', N.R. Srinivasan, *History
of the Indian Iron and Steel Company*, published by IISCO,
Burnpur, 1983, p. 121.

over by the central government in 1976 and formally nationalized in 1980.[153]

So ended the British managing agencies. By the early 1970s, the names that mattered in and around Dalhousie Square were the Birlas, Bangurs, Bajorias, Goenkas, Jalans, Kanorias, Kedias and Khaitans—the new plutocrats of the east.

How Long-term Debt Changed the Game

Until 1948, few if any industrial companies in India had access to long-term debt, primarily because it did not exist. Commercial banks engaged in bill discounting and working capital lending; none had either the capital or the risk-taking appetite to offer term loans over a tenor of seven to ten years to help large-scale industrialization. In fairness, they did not need to, because barring a few enterprises there were none that needed substantial chunks of capital for setting up and commissioning huge plants with a large component of machinery.

After Independence, the scale of new manufacturing units started increasing—first modestly and then rapidly during and following the Second Plan. The MNCs in India could finance significantly larger capital needs from their mother companies. Not so the Indian entrepreneurial groups. The investment needed for an aluminium plant was fifteen to twenty times higher than

[153] A.H. Antrobus, *History of Bird & Company*; and Tripathi and Jumani (2007), p. 178.

for a jute or cotton mill, and even higher when compared
with the investment required for collieries, tea plantations
and sugar mills. Equity alone no longer sufficed. For
one, Indian investors of the 1950s and 1960s neither had
the funds nor the kind of risk appetite to underwrite
public offers of the size of Rs 5 crore to Rs 20 crore. For
another, even if the investing public subscribed to such
large issues, the projects for which the money was raised
were not expected to be so profitable as to service the
higher cost of equity. For rapid industrialization, Indian
business groups needed long-term debt at affordable
rates of interest.

That happened with the coming of the nation's three
premier development finance institutions (DFIs), two
fully owned by the Government of India and all largely
funded by sovereign debt in the form of ad hoc treasury
bills that carried low rates of interest. The first DFI
was the Industrial Finance Corporation of India (IFCI)
which was formed in July 1948 in New Delhi. This
was followed by the Industrial Credit and Investment
Corporation of India (ICICI) in 1955 and then the
Industrial Development Bank of India (IDBI) in 1964,
both located in Bombay. The concept of DFIs focusing
on long-term loans for industrial and infrastructure
projects was not unique to India. After the World Bank
was established in 1948—itself a multilateral DFI—the
idea proliferated across various parts of the world such as
Germany, France, Italy, Yugoslavia, Japan, South Korea,
Indonesia, and even in major Latin American countries
like Brazil and Argentina.

To the corporate houses, IFCI, ICICI and IDBI were like manna from heaven. Larger ventures could now be envisaged. Accommodative finance was readily available, especially for activities and sectors that the government favoured. And while the loan covenants involved shares as security, these institutions were known to be considerate to their borrowers. Even in instances of loan defaults, rare was the case then, or now, where an Indian DFI invoked its covenant to sell the shares under its custody to a competitor. Rarer still was its taking over the hypothecated plant and equipment. Instead, loans were restructured as and when needed, prompting cheeky rogues to claim that rolling loans gathered no loss.

With the DFI being the Indian entrepreneur's friend and ally, large projects and expansion programmes could be now set up with a substantial component of long-term debt and a relatively low proportion of equity. The debt-equity ratio of major industrial projects was generally 2:1 and could climb to even 3:1. In plain English, with a 2:1 gearing, an entrepreneurial group could start a venture of Rs 15 crore with long-term debt of Rs 10 crore, which made the task of seeking Rs 5 crore of equity rather more simple. Besides, with own funds of, say, Rs 2 crore, the group could control 40 per cent of the equity. So long as the rest of the shareholders were sufficiently small and diverse and the DFI chairman suitably accommodating, Indian entrepreneurial groups could now control large companies despite having relatively little skin in the game. This was exactly what happened. Barring a few houses like the Birlas and the Bajaj group, which insisted upon majority ownership, most business groups began to control several large listed companies under their wing with equity ownership of 15 per cent or less. This was the case across most of the Tata group companies, the Mahindras, Mafatlals, Singhanias, Lalbhais, Wadias, the Thapars under Karam Chand's son, Lalit Mohan, and many others—including DCM and Escorts, where Bharat Ram, Charat Ram and H.P. Nanda suddenly discovered the risks of tiny holdings in the face of a hostile takeover from Swraj Paul in 1983.

The DFIs not only permitted Indian business groups to exercise hugely disproportionate control over substantially larger corporations than themselves, but also facilitated new ways for entrepreneurs to make money at the expense of the company and its shareholders. The favourite tactic, which started in the late 1960s and continued thereafter, was 'gold plating' of projects at the cost of debt. Essentially, sellers of imported machinery and capital goods were encouraged to over-invoice their bills, with the difference being paid into various accounts abroad. Since funds are fungible, an even more convenient strategy was to use part of the debt to finance the needs of other group businesses. Given the accounting standards of the time, rarely was such diversion discovered. Most importantly, the ready availability of concessional, long-term debt financed by a growing fiscal deficit of the Government of India reduced the need for using the legal structure of the 'managing agency' to exercise unequal control over corporate cash flows. Since what could be taken out through earlier managing agency contracts was now multiplied several times over, thanks to the generosity of the DFIs and their long-term loans, there seemed to be little use in continuing with the old system—especially for those business groups that were now active in the new industrial economy. Managing agencies were becoming dysfunctional. The clock was ticking. It needed a large scandal to accelerate their end. There were two.

Haridas Mundhra and Ramkrishna Dalmia

By the 1950s, Jawaharlal Nehru, all pro-socialist politicians in the country, the left, the fourth estate and India's intelligentsia had begun to dislike much of the private sector and the country's entrepreneurs. There were the odd exceptions such as the Tatas, who were appreciated as the right kind of nationalists, or the Lalbhais and Sarabhais who were looked up to by the Gujaratis. But in the brave new world of freedom and industrialization, the Marwaris in particular were looked down upon as an unprincipled, grubby, money-making lot—a perception that was strangely no different from the general view held by the British managing agencies in the colonial era. This noticeably worsened with the two big financial scandals of the time.

The first was the Mundhra affair.[154] Born into a trading family, Haridas Mundhra started as an agent for F. & C.

[154] The story of Haridas Mundhra is from three sources: G. Balachandran, *The Reserve Bank of India, 1951–1967*, Delhi, Oxford University Press, 1998; Nasir Tyabji, 'Private Industry and the Second Five Year Plan: The Mundhra Episode as

Osler (India) Limited, the Calcutta-based subsidiary of a well-known British light-bulb manufacturing company. Having made large wartime profits, he soon bought controlling stakes of this concern and then leveraged its cash flows to secure bank loans to purchase other firms, starting with two well-known engineering companies, Richardson & Cruddas in Bombay and Jessop in Calcutta. By using the free cash of these companies as well as the bank loans issued against his controlling stakes, Mundhra started his acquisition spree. He bought controlling interests in the Kanpur- and Calcutta-based British India Corporation (BIC) in 1955, whose stakes were then used to acquire 49 per cent of Turner Morrison, another British managing agency. Mundhra was an expert in snowballing and a master in manipulating share prices. One example was his acquisition of controlling interest in BIC by paying Rs 10–12 annas (i.e. Rs 10.75) per share. He then drove the share price up to almost Rs 14. Against these shares, valued at Rs 11 apiece as collateral, he obtained bank loans. In effect, he had financed the takeover entirely with borrowed funds.

All Ponzis have hard landings. Mundhra's happened by the end of 1956 when large bank borrowings coupled with declining share prices had put him in a nasty spot. Neither did he have the cash to take delivery of shares from brokers who had earlier helped finance his

---

Exemplar of Capitalist Myopia', *Economic & Political Weekly*, 7 August 2010, pp. 47–55; and Sucheta Dalal, *A.D. Shroff: Titan of Finance and Free Enterprise*, New Delhi, Viking, 2000.

transactions out of their own account, nor could he pay the additional margin money demanded by them as the price of most of his shares had slid south. There was a sense of imminent danger in Calcutta, with rumours flying around about Mundhra transacting in bogus shares. The word in town was that old-time Marwari businessmen who were now respected entrepreneurs with large managing agencies were deeply upset by the gunslinger actions of this seemingly uncouth parvenu, and that some of these businessmen were informing both the Reserve Bank of India and the ministry of finance of Mundhra's various chicaneries.[155]

As the RBI was beginning to tighten the screws, in stepped the government-owned Life Insurance Corporation of India (LIC). On 25 June 1957, either 'persuaded' or ordered by the finance minister T.T. Krishnamachari and his secretary H.M. Patel, LIC bought from Mundhra a mutually agreed-upon list of shares of six of his companies at the closing prices of the previous day. It was the Corporation's largest single-stock market

---

[155] Worried about what was going on, the Reserve Bank had conducted a series of inquiries. It was found that, 'Rumours abounded of shares in circulation of Richardson & Cruddas being in excess of the company's share capital. These rumours were confirmed in November 1957 when two banks reported to the [Reserve] Bank that they were in possession of duplicate shares of this company and of British India. Mundhra, one of these banks also discovered to its discomfiture, had pledged two sets of shares bearing the same serial numbers, neither of which was authentic, with two of its branches.' Balachandran (1998), Appendix D, 'The Bank and the Mundhra Affair'.

investment since its inception in 1955. LIC entered into
four more such transactions in September 1957.

Hell broke loose. From the treasury benches, Feroze
Gandhi, the Congress MP from Rae Bareilly and Nehru's
son-in-law, asked the government whether the newly
formed LIC had used the premiums of some 55 lakh
policyholders to buy up shares at higher-than-market
prices in the companies controlled by a notorious stock
market speculator named Haridas Mundhra. Humiliated
by his son-in-law, Nehru called upon a one-man
commission of inquiry headed by a noted retired Bombay
High Court judge, Justice M.C. Chagla, who concluded
his hearings in twenty-four days. He determined that
H.M. Patel and a couple of LIC officials may have
colluded to bail out Mundhra, which needed further
investigation. Much more important were Chagla's
views on the role of the finance minister. Regarding
Krishnamachari's attempt to distance himself from LIC's
decision by implying that the decision was taken by his
finance secretary, Chagla held that the minister must take
full responsibility for the actions of his subordinates and
should not be permitted to say that they did not reflect
his policy or had acted contrary to his directions. Hugely
embarrassed, Nehru forced Krishnamachari to resign in
February 1958.

Mundhra fell from grace and spent some time in jail.
A subsequent commission under Justice Vivian Bose
cleared H.M. Patel. But thanks to persistent press reports
of the time, most stridently in the *Blitz*, a Bombay tabloid
published by Russi Karanjia, Haridas Mundhra became a

publicly reviled figure, and dragged down with him many managing agencies who were tarred with the same brush.

The Mundhra episode paled into insignificance compared with the multiple underhand deals conducted by a much better known businessman, Ramkrishna Dalmia. A hugely clever Marwari who was born in Rajasthan, Dalmia moved to Calcutta at an early age. By his late teens, he had begun to speculate in various goods and bullion, steadily built a trading fortune and moved to Patna. Like many other Marwaris of the time, the young man got into industry during the inter-war years.

He started by setting up sugar mills across Bihar and the United Provinces. Dalmia's ambitions, however, went well beyond sugar. From a small town called Rohtas by the Sone river, not far from Patna, he got into cement. Within a short span of time, Dalmia Sahu Jain, the managing agency controlled by him and his son-in-law Shanti Prasad Jain, started building cement plants across India. They engaged in ruthless price wars with the country's major, the Associated Cement Companies of Bombay. Even that might have been tolerated by the wider business community as an embarrassing interlude. But Ramakrishna Dalmia wanted more, and would stop at nothing, least of all questionable inter-corporate financial deals.

By the early 1950s, Dalmia was the acquisition king of India. His group had taken over Bennett, Coleman & Company, publisher of the high-circulation *Times of India*; this was followed by purchase of three large jute mills of Andrew Yule; two more sugar mills and a flour mill under Govan Brothers; and a large stake in Punjab National Bank. He had diversified Rohtas Industries into various businesses including spun pipes, paper, chemicals and vanaspati; there was also a company called Bharat Insurance and an airline called Dalmia Jain Airways. Soon he represented the fourth largest business house in India.[156] Then came the shady deals.

Dalmia and his firms were found to be involved in several cases of large-scale tax evasion. There were massive fund transfers too, effected through complex interlocking of companies via three, possibly more, managing agencies. Dalmia Jain Airways was amalgamated with Dalmia Jain Aviation after suffering major losses, and its records were subsequently destroyed. Dalmia Cement and Paper Marketing Company, wholly owned by Ramkrishna, was structured so that all speculative profits accruing to various companies went to him, while losses were transferred to other group companies. Two profitable, listed cotton mills were forced to appoint closely held firms of the group as their sales agents, allowing these entities to skim off Rs 1.14 crore before terminating the sales contracts and putting the two mills under voluntary liquidation. Funds of Bharat Insurance were placed at the disposal of Dalmia's son-in-law so he could use them to acquire and retain control over other companies. None of these transgressions were comprehensively proven in the courts. What could be determined was the huge tax evasion by Ramkrishna Dalmia and some of his group

---

[156] Tripathi and Jumani (2007), pp. 165–66.

companies.[157] That led to a two-year jail sentence that Dalmia, in ways similar to today's well-connected felons, evaded by claiming to be sick and playing for time in various hospitals. However, his empire came to an end. When released, he tried to resume control of his group, only to be rebuffed by his son-in-law. Dalmia, a man who had eighteen children from six wives, disappeared from the scene altogether.

The Curtain Comes Down

It was one thing to have a much-disliked *arriviste* like Haridas Mundhra using the managing agency system for dabbling in shady transactions. It was quite another to have the fourth largest Indian business group of the 1950s to be found doing much worse. By the mid-1960s, both politicians and the middle class were fed up with the machinations of Indian businesses, especially managing agencies, which they believed were the root of all financial evil.[158]

[157] Nasir Tyabji, 'Of Traders, Usurers and British Capital: Managing Agencies and the Dalmia Jain Case', mimeo.

[158] One of the most damning indictments of the system came from an economist-cum-civil servant, R.K. Hazari, who was the chairman of the Central Government appointed Committee on Industrial Planning and Licencing Policy (1967) and was also the editor of the influential *Economic Weekly* from 1967 to 1969. In a data-packed article published in the journal in 1965, he wrote, 'Common impressions notwithstanding, the managing agency system [mostly Indian controlled] still predominates in the management of large public industrial

The institution was ripe for the dismantling at the time Indira Gandhi became prime minister in January 1966 after the death of Lal Bahadur Shastri in Tashkent. Mrs Gandhi bided her time. Following poor results for the Congress party in the 1967 general elections, she decisively moved to the left. That was when the managing agency system was struck its first blow. In 1967, Parliament approved section 324 of the Companies Act, 1956, under which managing agencies were to be terminated within a period of three years across five industries: jute, cotton, sugar, cement and paper.

Two years later, having fallen out with senior party leaders such as K. Kamaraj, Morarji Desai and S. Nijalingappa, and having being expelled from the Congress, Mrs Gandhi formed her own party. To the amazement of the old 'syndicate', she easily managed to get most of the Congress MPs on her side. With the 'progressives' under her wing, and assured of support from the left, Mrs Gandhi embarked on a series of radical measures such as the 1969 nationalization of fourteen

companies as it did before, only slightly less so. Law and policy have succeeded in somewhat restricting the managing agents' powers and reducing the remuneration paid to them but they still have a vast area of corporate activity under their managerial control'. He concluded, 'The rate at which the system is declining in importance is far too slow and gradual. A . . . killing of [such] rentier management is now necessary in the interest of developing a rational managerial set-up for large public industrial company.' See R.K. Hazari, 'Managing Agency System Far from Dead', *Economic Weekly*, July 10 1965, pp. 1101–1110.

large banks, the 1970 nationalization of coal mines and foreign oil companies, and abolition of the Privy Purse to rulers of the princely states.

In such an environment, it was but natural for the reign of the managing agencies to come to an end; which it formally did on 3 April 1970 under section 324A of the Companies Act. From that day onwards, the law stated that 'Notwithstanding anything contained in any other provision of this Act or in the memorandum or articles of association or in any contract to the contrary . . . a managing agent or secretaries and treasurers, the term of office of such managing agent or, as the case may be, the secretaries and treasurers shall expire, if it does not expire earlier.' Moreover, 'No company shall appoint or re-appoint any managing agent or secretaries and treasurers on or after the 3rd of April, 1970'.

Thus ended the institution that started with Dwarkanath Tagore in 1834. Or did it?

5

PLUS ÇA CHANGE . . .

The French have a maxim or two for everything under the sun. Coined by Jean-Baptiste Alphonse Karr in 1849, *'Plus ça change, plus c'est la même chose'* loosely means 'The more things change, the more they stay the same'. It is certainly true for managing agencies. In one avatar or the other, the basic structure and operational form of the managing agency proliferated throughout pre- and post-World War II Asia. Moreover, its formal abolition in India in April 1970 did little to change its modus operandi. Many entrepreneurial groups created other organizational forms and skilfully used different helpful sections of the Companies Act, 1956, to continue exercising disproportionate control over the cash flows of the many companies promoted by them, well in excess of their shareholding rights. Until the beginning of the twenty-first century, exerting unequal control via managing agency-like structures was the norm. Indeed, with some notable exceptions, it continues even today. But first, a brief tale of corporate control in other parts of Asia.

Japan: Zaibatsus and Keiretsus

Literally meaning financial cliques or groups, the zaibatsus were large family-controlled monopolies across various sectors. Predating but becoming prominent with the Meiji Restoration of 1868 and then far more significant during Japan's subsequent industrialisation and military campaigns up to the end of World War II, a typical zaibatsu had a holding company on top and a wholly owned bank to provide the necessary finance, with several industrial and other subsidiaries that dominated specific markets either solely or through another array of second-level subsidiary enterprises. By 1937, the big four zaibatsus were Mitsui, Mitsubishi, Sumitomo and Yasuda which comprised 15 per cent of the combined paid-up capital of all Japanese joint-stock companies, and accounted for direct control over most of the country's mining, chemical, metals, machinery and capital goods industries, textiles as well as much of its commercial merchant fleet.[159] In addition to the big four were others such as Okura, Furukawa, Kuhara, Suzuki, Fujita, Asano, Nissan (derived from Nippon Sangyo), Nitchitsu and Mori.

[159] Juro Hashimoto, 'The Rise of Big Business', in T. Nakamura and K. Odaka (eds.), *Economic History of Japan, 1914–1955*, Oxford University Press, 1999, pp. 217–18.

Akin to managing agencies, while there was public shareholding in the subsidiary companies, the holding firms remained resolutely private, secretive to the extreme, dominated by the family and its trusted lieutenants and connected to all arms of the Imperial government. Also similar to managing agencies, instead of specializing in one industry or two like most US conglomerates did in the first half of the twentieth century, the zaibatsus grew through agglomeration of many different businesses, with the family-run holding company controlling banks, financial enterprises, manufacturing, mining, shipping and trading. These core companies in turn controlled other subsidiaries. Interlocking directorships and lifetime employment encouraged group solidarity. All these factors gave each zaibatsu a seemingly feudal character, with thousands of its workers pledging allegiance to the house.

After Japan formally signed its instruments of surrender in September 1945, General Douglas MacArthur, the supreme commander of the Allied forces in the country, was determined to end all institutions that might again promote militarism. Among these were the zaibatsus. On 6 November 1945, barely two months after the surrender, MacArthur ordered their breakup. Some of the heads of families were removed from their posts and jailed; corporate use of their names was banned; and shares of their holding companies were sold to the public. Then came the cold war. Suddenly, Japan became geopolitically important to the US. So, of the 300-odd zaibatsu controlled companies identified for breakup, only twenty were dismantled. Soon enough, the holding company shares were bought by banks and big businesses, which began to put the groupings together again.[160] That started the keiretsus, which have been an integral part of the business landscape of Japan since the 1950s.

Meaning a 'system' or a 'series', a keiretsu represents a set of companies with interlocking business relationships and shareholdings, but centred on a core bank which is also the largest shareholder of the key group entities. Some economists and corporate specialists have claimed that having a main bank in each keiretsu as both lender and main shareholder insulates each firm under it from stock market fluctuations, prevents hostile takeovers and allows for long-term corporate planning.[161] Frankly, the real reason for keiretsus and their main banks is that these are so uniquely Japanese—a culture that prides on quiet control and long-term order. Again, there is a striking similarity with managing agencies, especially those of the large Indian business houses. In the 1960s, the board of the Bank of Baroda had R.D. Birla, Naval Tata, Rasesh Mafatlal, K.P. Goenka and R.D. Bangur, whose companies

[160] *The Economist*, Millennium Issue, 23 December 1999.
[161] See, for instance, Stephen D. Prowse, 'Institutional Investment Patterns and Corporate Financial Behavior in the United States and Japan', *Journal of Financial Economics*, Vol. 27, 1990, pp. 43–66; Takeo Hoshi, 'The Economic Role of Corporate Grouping and the Main Bank System', in M. Aoki and R. Dore, *The Japanese Firm: The Sources of Competitive Strength*, Oxford University Press, 1994, pp. 285–309; and M. Aoki, 'The Japanese Firm as a System of Attributes', *ibid.*, pp. 11–40.

were preferred customers for bank loans; the Central Bank of India was, for all intents and purposes, the resident bank of the Tatas with Sir Homi Mody, C.H. Bhabha and Nani Palkhivala on the board; the Indian Bank was for and of the Chettiars; and the United Commercial Bank, controlled by Birla till its nationalization, served the Marwaris of Calcutta. Many general insurance companies were also under de facto control of the Birla, Tatas, Singhanias, Karam Chand Thapar and others.

The eight major post-war keiretsus are: Mitsubishi, Mitsui, Sumitomo, Fuyo, Dai-ichi Kangyo, Sanwa, Tokai and IBJ. The top three, Mitsubishi, Mitsui and Sumitomo, were among the big four zaibatsus in the pre-World War II era. Consider as an example Mitsubishi's span of control. It has as the lead bank the Mitsubishi Bank which became the Bank of Tokyo-Mitsubishi from 1996; and in varying degrees it controls Tokio Marine and Fire Insurance; Kirin Brewery; Mitsubishi Electric; Mitsubishi Motors; Mitsubishi Heavy Industries; Nippon Oil; Nikon; Mitsubishi Chemical; Mitsubishi Rayon; Asahi Glass; Mitsubishi Paper; Mitsubishi Steel; and the global shipping giant Nippon Yusen Kaisha or NYK. This is a very abridged list. The situation is similar for Mitsui, Sumitomo and the other majors. Here again is the story of large groups controlling hundreds of major and minor companies through their so-called 'main banks' and by complex interlocking of shares as well as directors. These are but managing agencies by another name—larger, global and more successful—a fact that would have impressed Dwarkanath to no end.

South Korea: Chaebols

In Korean, '*chae*' denotes wealth or property and '*bol*' group or clan. Together, it is perfectly apposite for the nation's major business conglomerates such as Hyundai, Samsung, LG, Hanjin or Doosan—global entities owning several enterprises that are generally controlled by a chairman who is typically the head of the business family and has power over most if not all substantive decisions.

More than the zaibatsus are keiretsus, growth of the chaebols has much to do with active financial assistance and explicit encouragement of successive national governments after the seizure of power by the military general Park Chung Hee in 1961. In his First Five Year Plan, President Park set out a policy of rapid industrialization. Unlike Nehru who opted for state-owned enterprises as the vehicles of heavy industrialization, Park did so by setting the direction of investment and then helping to promote large businesses in the private sector which were aided by government guaranteed loans from foreign and domestic banks. Besides, Park's focus was on export-led growth, which not only encouraged enterprises under the chaebols to be globally competitive in manufacturing practices and product quality but also earned much needed foreign exchange to service international loans and build reserves to finance further chaebol-driven export-led growth. President Park was assassinated in 1979, but the national policy to have export-led industrial growth driven by development finance and through various chaebols continued with his successors. Thanks to unrestricted government assistance to the chosen ones, the chaebols grew to being multinational conglomerates by the late 1980s; managed to withstand the Asian financial crisis of 1997–98; and after further consolidation, rank among some of the international giants of today.[162]

Though similar in some areas, chaebols are far more controlled by their founding entrepreneurial families than keiretsus; and, therefore, on the boards and at higher echelons of management, tend to have greater family presence. They are also more centralized in ownership, and rely on complex interlocking ownership. The family owning a chaebol uses its own stakes, those of family-owned charities and of senior managers from subsidiaries to control a small number of publicly listed companies which control other companies that further control subsidiaries. A major structural difference is that, unlike keiretsus, chaebols do not have their own banks or financial institutions which, in their early stages, made them more dependent on the goodwill of successive Korean governments, state sponsored DFIs and government-backed loans and guarantees.

Are chaebols akin to managing agencies? Indeed so. The promoting family, through interconnected companies,

---

[162] An example suffices to demonstrate the scale of some of the large chaebols. For the year ended 31 December 2014, Samsung Electronic Company Limited's consolidated revenue was almost US$196 billion; it earned an operating profit of 12 per cent on revenue, or US$23 billion; its post-tax net profit was US$22 billion; and cash and cash equivalents sitting on its balance sheet were US$16 billion. Samsung Electronics, *Annual Report 2014*.

interlocking share ownership and a common pool of loyal directors control a vast number of companies with relatively little direct ownership. Like Indian entrepreneurs and managing agencies in the era of DFIs such as IFCI, ICICI and IDBI, these entities depended upon state-directed financial support for industrialization to grow their empires with relatively little risk capital, and even less so out of their own pockets. The families had various types of arrangements with the companies that they controlled which gave them access to different types of cash flows that were far in excess of their actual direct and indirect share ownership. The entrepreneurial group's control was absolute over its companies—arguably far more so than Indian managing agencies. If there was a heaven sent nation for creating highly concentrated private business groups that were intensely loyal to the state, it was South Korea. Instead of dealing with Nehru's socialism and dodging Indira Gandhi's leftism, licences, controls and rampant nationalization, how much a G.D. Birla or a J.R.D. Tata would have loved to operate in a country like that!

Hong Kong: Taipans, Old and New

William Jardine was born in Scotland in 1784. After graduating in medicine from Edinburgh University, he became a surgeon on the ships of the East India Company that plied between India, China and London. As a ship's senior officer, Jardine was allocated cargo space equal to two chests to conduct his own business. Once he got into trading, Jardine discovered that selling Malwa and Ghazipur opium in Canton was far more profitable than dispensing medicine to a ship's crew. After a long opium trading partnership with Jamsetjee Jeejeebhoy, he encountered James Matheson, another Scot, a dozen years younger than him, who was actively involved in Canton selling opium and buying tea with a dynamic and profitable agency house called Yrissari & Company. After the death of Xavier de Yrissari, and with the shares of the founder being willed to him, Matheson sought out Jardine who was only too willing to have him as a partner. Thus started Jardine, Matheson & Company. It soon became the largest smuggler of opium into China and the largest exporter of tea from Canton to England.

In 1839, after the Chinese emperor sent a senior mandarin, Lin Zexu, to Canton to stop the opium trade altogether, Lin had the temerity to confiscate and destroy over 20,000 crates of opium, much of which belonged to Jardine, Matheson & Company. William Jardine, then in London, prevailed upon the foreign secretary, Lord Palmerston to wage war on China. The Opium War followed soon after. In 1842, the Treaty of Nanking forced the opening of five Chinese ports including Shanghai, provided indemnification for the opium destroyed and completed the formal acquisition of Hong Kong. The China trade grew in leaps and bounds driven by opium and tea, and with it the fortunes of Jardine, Matheson & Company, now by far the largest British trading firm in the region and locally known as the 'Princely Hong'. Soon enough, Jardine, Matheson moved its headquarters to Hong Kong, where it stands today; and carrying on a long Chinese tradition, the head of the group is called the taipan.

The enterprise was huge by the end of the nineteenth century and grew further still until the beginning of World War II. It had ten branches in China, one in Japan, and a host of profitable subsidiaries that included the island's largest land agency, wharves and godowns, steam navigation and shipping, the Star Ferry, Hong King Tramways, cold storages, breweries, cotton mills, dairy farms and various fire and general insurance companies. It expanded further in the 1950s and 1960s. Controlled by the Keswick family, descendants of Jardine's sister, it set up the Mandarin Oriental Hotel, the Wellcome supermarket chain, acquired Gammon Construction, created Jardine Motors as the sellers of Mercedes Benz and other high-end cars, and founded Jardine Fleming, an investment banking and share broking house that became the largest in Hong Kong.

Jardine, Matheson & Company was a quintessential managing agency. Secretive and family controlled, it leveraged its entrepreneurial skills and long-nurtured China and London contacts to promote one company after another across a wide range of activities, while ensuring control over various subsidiaries often with relatively low shareholding. That almost caused it grief in 1977 when Li Ka-Shing of Cheung Kong Holdings made a successful bid to develop lucrative land sites above the Central and Admiralty metro stations in his effort to challenge Jardine, Matheson as the premier property developer in Hong Kong.

Born in 1928, Li Ka-Shing is probably the richest man in Asia and the most powerful businessman in Hong Kong. Starting with a plastic company in 1950, he became the largest and most profitable supplier of plastic flowers in Asia. He used free cash from the plastic flowers business to purchase properties at low prices during the riots of 1967, whose values subsequently rose many fold. This was the start of Cheung Kong Holdings which was listed on the Hong Kong Stock Exchange in 1972. Cheung Kong soon became the largest property developer in Hong Kong. With property profits and helpful bank finance, Li Ka-Shing used Cheung Kong to make his largest acquisition in 1979, an entity that became the group's flagship company, Hutchison Whampoa, which was involved in multiple activities dominated by global container port facilities in Hong Kong, Vancouver, China, Rotterdam and elsewhere. He then used the cash flows of Hutchison Whampoa to acquire the A.S. Watson group, a retail chain of over 7,800 stores worldwide. Like all managing agencies, the group is carefully structured to retain disproportionate control without incurring the cost of owning an equivalent economic interest. As expected, the separation between control and interest is realized through cross-holdings, multiple pyramid structures and the issuing of dual-class equities.

A Popular Form, Indeed

Managing agency type structures abound elsewhere. In Mexico, through Grupo Carso, the businesses controlled by the world's richest man, Carlos Slim, span telecom, manufacturing, chemicals, real estate, airlines, media, mining, oil, hospitality, technology, retailing and financial services.[163] LVMH, the Paris-based luxury goods giant which has some sixty subsidiaries is controlled by Bernard Arnault and his family through Christian Dior.[164] In Spain, the family of Emilio Botín (1934–2014), now led by his daughter Ana Patricia controls Grupo Santander and, through it, Banco Santander with over 14,000 bank branches over Europe, Latin America and the US. The family of Lazaro de Mello Brandao controls one of Brazil's major financial services conglomerate, BBD Participacoes, while that of Abilio dos Santos Diniz controls the country's largest retail chain, Wilkes Participacoes. The Soriano family of Philippines controls the San Miguel group, which is involved in beer, food, packaging, properties, oil and energy businesses. It owned a 49 per cent stake in Philippines Airlines which was subsequently sold for a hefty profit to another business house. The list goes on.

Why is the essential form of a managing agency so popular across various parts of the world? There are five main reasons. First, and perhaps the most

[163] According to *Forbes*, Slim's net worth as of March 2015 was estimated at US$ 71 billion.

[164] The companies under LVMH represent the *crème de la crème* of luxury: Hennessy, Moet & Chandon, Krug, Dom Perignon, Veuve Clicquot, Ardbeg, Glenmorangie, Dior, Donna Karan, Givenchy, Fendi, Kenzo, Louis Vuitton, Thomas Pink, Bulgari, Hublot, TAG Heuer, not to mention retail outlets like Sephora and Le Bon Marché.

important, is the limited supply of entrepreneurship. Be it in colonial India or even after Independence right up to the 1980s, in Japan from the Meiji Restoration up to World War II and then till recent times, or South Korea since the 1960s, or Hong Kong, Mexico, Spain, Brazil or the Philippines, entrepreneurship was limited to the relatively few. Such people took the risks; and having done so, wanted to put in place structures that could preserve their control over the businesses. The managing agency, in whatever name or form, not only provided just the right kind of arrangement but also ensured that the promoters' cash flow entitlements far exceeded their pure shareholding rights.

Second, the system was maintained and perpetuated thanks to the acceptance of the vast body of minority shareholders. So long as they received suitable dividends year after year and the share prices continued to appreciate in a reasonably sustained fashion, they were content to let the managing agencies or the controlling enterprises run the business without any hard questioning at the annual general meetings (AGMs) or any form of institutional investor activism that one now sees in the US, the UK and occasionally in India.[165] The general philosophy was: Am I being rewarded sufficiently? Yes. Then I support the company and its promoters and let it be.

[165] In the past, Japanese corporations used to employ the services of gangster from different *yakuza* syndicates to act as bouncers at their AGMs. The firms still pursue a unique way of avoiding shareholder activism by holding almost all Japanese AGMs on the same date.

Third, and this was particularly true after World War II, the business conglomerates secured considerable support from state-sponsored or state-directed DFIs. Whether it be driven by the maxim of rapid industrialisation starting with the Second Five Year Plan in India or the First Plan under President Park in Korea, or arising out of the need to rebuild war-torn Europe and Japan, or economic nationalism in Brazil, Mexico, Indonesia and Malaysia, countries set up one DFI after another to advance long-term loans at concessional rates of interest to build industry. Entrepreneurial groups used this facility in plenty: it not only reduced the pressure on higher cost equity to fund large projects but also gave them a cash flow cushion since pliable DFIs were often 'instructed' to restructure loans when entrepreneurs faced difficulties in repayment. Besides, unlike working capital which, if turned off, could badly affect day-to-day operations, term loans were sticky; and in many countries, poor bankruptcy laws and procedures made it virtually impossible to attach and transfer hypothecated plant and machinery in the event of default. DFIs loans, therefore, generously widened the field of play without constraining the control structures that the entrepreneurial groups foisted on their businesses.

Fourth, corporate laws were peppered with convenient loopholes. In the Indian context, some of these will be touched upon in the next section. Accounting standards and disclosures were inadequate, often notoriously poor, across most parts of the world right up to the 1990s, which allowed promoters and management to shroud many a transaction that benefited the closely held entities at the expense of the public corporation. Finally, in many countries such as Japan, South Korea, Mexico, Brazil, India, Indonesia, Malaysia and Hong Kong, the major entrepreneurial groups enjoyed close proximity to, and patronage of, successive governments. Rules could be subtly amended, interpretations altered and unwritten directions given to assist the entrepreneurs. With all these five factors in play, who could have possibly expected otherwise?

. . . Plus c'est la même chose

The King is dead. Long live the King. In purely legal terms, managing agencies were formally abolished in India in 1970. But the practices have continued, sometimes on a scale grander than ever before. As stated in Chapter 1, the crux of the issue is agency costs. Except in rare cases and in the absence of strong countervailing power of the financial press and institutional investors, promoters are loathe to limit their share of corporate cash flows to only their return on equity. After all, they and their managers control and run their companies and know much more about the intricacies of their businesses than others. Indeed, they make more efforts than the outside shareholders. Hence, subject to keeping the shareholders content, why should they not get more out of their companies than the others? And maintain control as long as they wish to?

Hence, even after abolition of managing agencies, most entrepreneurial groups in India have designed a complex weave of private limited companies around each major listed entity that they control. Reliance Industries under Mukesh Ambani and the Reliance ADAG under his younger brother Anil probably head this list. Though others may not have as many privately held companies nestled under their group umbrellas, the practice is pervasive. Through cross-holdings and interlocking of interests, these private entities serve as instruments of control of—and recipients of cash flows from—the publicly held and listed companies.

The Companies Act, 1956, allowed for various such forms of transfer of funds. For instance, section 294 permitted the appointment of sole selling agents, on each occasion for a period of five years, by a resolution that needed to be passed by shareholders present and voting at the company's AGM. With the promoters and their associates accounting for the bulk of equity among the shareholders present at any AGM, such contracts were routinely passed every five years. And since, more often than not, the sole selling agent was a privately held company of the promoters, commissions on such sales, typically varying between 2.5 per cent to 5 per cent depending on the product and its volume, would accrue to the promoter group—no different from what the managing agencies practised before 1970.

Similarly, section 370 allowed companies to advance loans to other group entities via passing a special resolution in the AGM, provided the loan did not exceed the aggregate value of paid-up share capital and free reserves. Section 372A permitted companies to make inter-corporate loans and investments up to 60 per cent of its paid-up capital and free reserves, or 100 per cent of its free reserves, whichever was greater. While facilitating inter-corporate investments such as purchase of shares of related companies, section 372A created a perfect avenue for transferring shareholder funds of the purchasing company to less-regulated private enterprise and then to other pockets. This was, and continues to be, a way of shifting funds from listed companies which come under greater investor and regulatory scrutiny to various unlisted, privately held special purpose vehicles (SPVs), particularly in infrastructure. There were many other such provisions in the Companies Act, 1956. Together, these created opportunities to transfer funds and retain control of various enterprises under a group much in the way of managing agencies.

There have been other methods as well. Section 79 of the Companies Act permitted the issuing of additional shares at a discount subject to the approval of shareholders at the AGM. After the advent of economic liberalization in 1991 which increased the foreign shareholding ceiling for many industries, several MNCs including Hindustan Lever immediately got this passed by the shareholders and issued shares at steep discounts to the prevailing price to the foreign promoter group. While legally permissible, it was a palpably wrong act of corporate governance for it effectively treated one class of shareholders, the promoters, as special while the others were children of lesser gods. Thankfully, it was banned after a few years. But by then the horses had bolted.

Another practice uncannily similar to that used by managing agencies was the approval of various forms of commissions on sales, payable directly to the entrepreneurial group. Tata Sons started charging a fee of 0.25 per cent on sales across all its group entities for use of the 'Tata' brand. Soon Nusli Wadia followed with an identical fee being levied upon its group companies, Bombay Dyeing and Britannia Industries. The Swiss giant ABB got the board of ABB India to approve a levy of 2 per cent on sales as did Castrol on Castrol India Limited. Bosch charged 1.7 per cent on Bosch India. Asahi India Glass paid a brand royalty of 1.9 per cent of the turnover. Hindustan Lever paid 1.4 per cent; Nestle India 3.5 per cent; Maruti Suzuki 5.5 per cent; Colgate Palmolive India in excess of 5 per cent; Procter & Gamble Hygiene almost 5 per cent; and Glaxo Smithkline Consumer over 3 per cent. While some of these had a so-called 'technological fee' component, in essence such arrangements were similar to those between managing agencies and their promoted companies. No doubt, these were approved by the board of directors of the paying companies. But that was because the promoters dominated these boards and also because non-executive and apparently independent directors assented without ever thinking that they were fiduciaries of minority shareholders. They were, as many still are, decorative items not dissimilar to parsley on the fish.

For all these shortcoming, things did start to change for the better after the 1990s. The financial press and television became more informed. Companies found themselves being publicly embarrassed by revelations of their mischiefs. The more modern entrepreneurs realized that it is better to run a clean business and benefit from the additional share value that good reputation can bring than to squirrel whatever, wherever and whenever they could. A modern corporate governance code for listed companies was announced by the Securities and Exchange Board of India (SEBI). At the same time, led by companies such as Infosys, Wipro, TCS, HDFC, HDFC Bank, ICICI Bank, Axis Bank, Bajaj Auto, Dr Reddy's Laboratories, Cipla, Sun Pharma, Mahindra & Mahindra, Godrej Consumer Products, there started a distinct groundswell in favour of probity and clean business.

Then came Satyam. On 7 January 2009 at 10.53 a.m., a fax from B. Ramalinga Raju, chairman of Satyam Computer Services Limited, to its board of directors, the chairman of the SEBI and the stock exchanges was like a megaton bomb exploding in the face of corporate India. He admitted to multiple misdeeds which were huge in scale and unheard of till then. The cooking of the books was staggering. Raju and his accomplices inflated Satyam's cash and bank balance as on 30 September 2008 by a colossal Rs 5,040 crore. According to the official balance sheet, Satyam's cash and bank balance was Rs 5,361 crore. After subtracting the Rs 5,040 crore fudge, the real balance was just Rs 321 crore. Yet it had proposed to purchase two group companies, Maytas Properties and Maytas Infrastructure, for US$1.6 billion (Rs 7,700 crore)—a deal which while assented to by a pliant board was turned down in a fierce conference call by all institutional investors. In Raju's pathetic confession, 'The aborted Maytas acquisition deal was the last attempt to fill the fictitious assets with real ones'. A desperately cash strapped company was fudging its books to show non-existent funds to make an acquisition that it was in no position to pay for, for it to command valuable real estate which it could then show as fungible assets on its balance sheet! That wasn't all. Satyam claimed non-existent accrued interest of Rs 376 crore and increased current assets by overstating debtors dues by Rs 490 crore.[166]

The consequence of Satyam has been enormous. In the public eye, all of corporate India has been tarred by this single monumental scandal. In response to Satyam, the Parliament passed the new Companies Act, 2013. While this latest edition has many improvements over the various amended versions of the act of 1956, Satyam has led to it containing several draconian provisions—negative, harsh and dysfunctional enough to sometimes throw the baby out with the bath water. In more ways than one, it is a legal remaking of the control raj. Unfortunately, its proponents say, 'After Satyam, you asked for it.'

Having said so, there is no denying that India has listed enterprises which are noted for their sound corporate governance practices. Companies such as TCS, Infosys and Wipro in the information technology sector; Sun Pharma, Dr Reddy's, Cipla and Lupin in pharmaceuticals; HDFC, HDFC Bank, Axis Bank, Kotak Mahindra, ICICI Bank, IDFC and Bajaj Finance in banking and financial

[166] Omkar Goswami, 'Lessons from Satyam', *Hindustan Times*, January 2009.

services; Bajaj Auto, Tata Motors and Hero Motocorp in automobiles and two-wheelers; Mahindra & Mahindra in automobiles and tractors; and some others now lead the way in transparency, corporate governance and financial as well as non-financial disclosures. Though not enough, boards, too, have improved with more diligent independent directors who do their homework and, while supporting management where needed, focus on the interests of minority shareholders.

However, these changes are still too few and far between for comfort. Even today, despite significant improvements in financial reporting standards, a large number of public limited companies, listed or otherwise, practice questionable to average corporate governance and dodgy accounting. Many still follow the consecrated methods of the managing agencies and do so because the promoters genuinely believe that, by virtue of their risk taking, their cash flow dues must necessarily exceed their rights as principal shareholders. Optimists will say that things will change for the better—as these indeed have over the last two decades. Pessimists will disagree, claiming that the kernel of agency costs will always come into play and forever encourage entrepreneurs to corner more than what is warranted.

Perhaps not. Perhaps the consequences of modern law, better stock exchange regulation and practices, superior corporate governance in substance rather than mere form and the power of quick reportage by a vigilant press will turn the tide. Time will tell. Hopefully an equally exciting yet better tale than what you have read in this book.

ACKNOWLEDGEMENTS

Since my youth, while swotting at various libraries and archives at Oxford, Cambridge, Calcutta and New Delhi, I have been fascinated by managing agencies. Not just for how these institutions oversaw and parented the growth of industrialization and the corporate world in India, or how they strove to maintain control despite thin ownership, but also for the roles of the main actors in the drama: Dwarkanath Tagore, Jamsetji Tata and his son Dorabji, David Yule, Thomas Catto, Edward and Paul Benthall, Ghanshyamdas Birla, Keshav Prasad Goenka, Kasturbhai Lalbhai, Walchand Hirachand and others who fashioned today's corporate India. I am indebted to the Inlaks Foundation for a generous scholarship in 1979–82 to do my research and DPhil at Oxford, and to the libraries and archives where each day I found at least one quotable gem.

In no less a measure, I benefited from teaching and researching at several excellent institutions in India and abroad, and from interacting with the faculty and clever graduate students alike to sharpen my ideas over the years.

My stint as editor of *Business India*, the most respected business fortnightly of the time, made me understand more of the entrepreneurial world.

Since then, much has been learnt at a granular level by working at the Confederation of Indian Industry for half a dozen years, and by serving as an independent director on the boards of major listed companies such as Infosys, Dr Reddy's Laboratories, Cairn India, Ambuja Cement, IDFC, Crompton Greaves, Godrej Consumer Products and Bajaj Finance. All this, better than any tome you might choose to read, teaches you more about how firms actually work and how entrepreneurs think. I am, therefore, no less grateful for this experience, which has been a part of my curricular life for almost a decade-and-a-half; so too for the stints as adviser to many companies and their boards, where I have learnt more than opined.

My thanks to Gita Piramal, a superb business historian—and a friend since the mid 1980s—with whom I have had innumerable conversations and from whom I have learnt a great deal. I must also thank Gurcharan Das for prompting me to write this book. It was always on my mind, but without Gurcharan's offer, prodding and incisive comments, it would have just remained there. Udayan Mitra and Paloma Dutta of Penguin Random House India have been very helpful with the text and other suggestions; and Udayan has quietly borne with, and often astutely deflected, my numerous objections.

Finally, to Radhika—not just for this book, but for making so many wonderful things happen to the both us. And to young Samar for unbounded joy.

SELECT BIBLIOGRAPHY

Aoki, M., 'The Japanese Firm as a System of Attributes' in M. Aoki and R. Dore, *The Japanese Firm: The Sources of Competitive Strength*, Oxford University Press, 1994, pp. 11–40.

Bagchi, Amiya K., *Private Investment in India, 1900–1939*, Cambridge University Press, Cambridge, 1972.

Bagchi, Amiya K., *The Presidency Banks and the Indian Economy, 1876–1914*, Oxford University Press, Calcutta, 1989.

Balachandran, G., *The Reserve Bank of India, 1951–1967*, Oxford University Press, Delhi, 1998.

Bank of England, Three Centuries of Data, electronic database.

Capital, a Calcutta-based business magazine, 16 November 1933.

CBJA (Calcutta Baled Jute Association), *Report of the Committee 1908–09*, Calcutta, 1909.

CSAS (Centre for South Asian Studies), University of Cambridge, *Papers of Sir Edward Benthall*.

Dalal, Sucheta, *A.D. Shroff: Titan of Finance and Free Enterprise*, Viking, New Delhi, 2000.

Damodaran, Harish, *India's New Capitalists: Caste, Business and Industry in a Modern Nation*, Permanent Black, 2008.

Desai, Ashok V., 'The Origins of Parsi Enterprise', *IESHR*, Vol. 5(4), reprinted in Rajat K. Ray (ed.), *Entrepreneurship and Industry in India, 1800–1947*, Oxford University Press, Delhi, 1992.

Economic and Political Weekly (EPW) Research Foundation, *India Time Series*, a digital database on the Indian economy.

en.wikipedia.org/wiki/Carlos_Slim.

en.wikipedia.org/wiki/Cheung_Kong_Holdings.

en.wikipedia.org/wiki/Hutchison_Whampoa

en.wikipedia.org/wiki/Jardine_Matheson.

en.wikipedia.org/wiki/Jwala_Prasad_Srivastava.

en.wikipedia.org/wiki/Kasturbhai_Lalbhai.

en.wikipedia.org/wiki/Lala_Shri_Ram.

en.wikipedia.org/wiki/Li_Ka-shing.

en.wikipedia.org/wiki/LVMH.

en.wikipedia.org/wiki/Murugappa_Group.

en.wikipedia.org/wiki/San_Miguel_Corporation.

en.wikipedia.org/wiki/Santander_Group.

Fay, Peter Ward, *The Opium War, 1840–42*, University of North Carolina Press, 1975.

Goswami, Omkar, 'Collaboration and Conflict: Indian and European Capitalists and the Jute Economy of Bengal', *Indian Economic and Social History Review (IESHR)*, 19(2), 1982, pp. 141–79 .

Goswami, Omkar, '*Sahibs, Babus* and *Banias*: Changes in Industrial Control in Eastern India, 1918–1950', *The Journal of Asian Studies*, 48(2), 1989, pp. 289–309.

Goswami, Omkar, *Industry, Trade and Peasant Society: The Jute Economy of Eastern India, 1900–1947*, Oxford University Press, Delhi, 1991.

Goswami, Omkar, 'Lessons from Satyam', *Hindustan Times*, January 2009.

Government of Bengal, Commerce Department, Commerce Branch.

Government of Bengal, *Report of the Bengal Jute Enquiry Committee (Fawcus)*, Alipore, 1940.

Government of India, *Census of India 1911*, Vol. I (1)

Government of India, *The Second Five Year Plan (1956–61)*, New Delhi.

Harrison, Godfrey, *Bird and Company of Calcutta, 1864–1964*, Calcutta, 1964.

Hashimoto, Juro, 'The Rise of Big Business', in T. Nakamura and K. Odaka (eds.), *Economic History of Japan, 1914–1955*, Oxford University Press, 1999, pp. 217–18.

Hazari, R.K., 'Managing Agency System Far from Dead', *Economic Weekly*, 10 July 1965, pp. 1101–1110.

Hindustan Standard, a Calcutta-based English daily, 1 January 1938.

Hobsbawm, Eric, *The Age of Empire, 1875–1914*, Vintage Books, 1989.

Hoshi, Takeo, 'The Economic Role of Corporate Grouping and the Main Bank System', in M. Aoki and

R. Dore, *The Japanese Firm: The Sources of Competitive Strength*, Oxford University Press, 1994, pp. 285–309.

IJMA, *Report of the Committee,* successive years.

Investor's India Year Book (IIYB), successive annual issues, Place, Siddons & Gough, Calcutta.

Jensen, Michael C. and William H. Meckling, 'Theory of the Firm: Managerial Behavior, Agency Costs and Ownership Structure', *Journal of Financial Economics,* 3(4), October 1976, pp. 305–360.

Jones, Stephanie, *Merchants of the Raj: British Managing Agency Houses in Calcutta Yesterday and Today*, MacMillan Press, 1992.

Kling, Blair B., *Partner in Empire: Dwarkanath Tagore and the Age of Enterprise in Eastern India,* University of California Press, 1976.

Kling, Blair B., 'The Origin of the Managing Agency System in India', *Journal of Asian Studies,* University of California Press, XXVI(1), November 1969, reprinted in Rajat K. Ray (ed.), *Entrepreneurship and Industry in India, 1800–1947,* Oxford University Press, Delhi, 1992, pp. 83–98.

Kudaisya, Medha M., *The Life and Times of G.D. Birla,* Oxford University Press, 2003.

Lethbridge, Roper KCIE, *The Golden Book of India: A Genealogical and Biographical Dictionary of the Ruling Princes, Chiefs, Nobles and Other Personages, Titled or Decorated, of the British Empire,* 1893, re-published by Aakar Books.

Lokanathan, P.S, *Industrial Organisation in India,* Allen & Unwin, London, 1935.

Marshall, Peter, *East Indian Fortunes: The British in Bengal in the Eighteenth Century*, Clarendon Press, Oxford, 1976.

Misra, Maria, *Business, Race, and Politics in British India c.1850–1960*, Clarendon Press, Oxford, 1990.

Mohan, Rakesh and Vandana Aggarwal, 'Commands and Control: Planning for Indian Industrial Development, 1951–1990', *Journal of Comparative Economics*, Vol. 14, 1990, pp. 683–84.

Mukherjee, Rudrangshu, *Nehru & Bose: Parallel Lives*, Penguin/Viking, 2014.

Piramal, Gita, *Business Legends*, Viking, 1998.

Piramal, Gita, *Kamalnayan Bajaj: Architect of the Bajaj Group*, Kamalnayan Bajaj Charitable Trust, 2015.

Prowse, Stephen D., 'Institutional Investment Patterns and Corporate Financial Behavior in the United States and Japan', *Journal of Financial Economics*, Vol. 27, 1990, pp. 43–66.

Samsung Electronics, *Annual Report 2014*.

Sanyal, Amal, 'The Curious Case of the Bombay Plan', *Contemporary Issues and Ideas in Social Sciences*, June 2010, mimeo.

Simmons, Colin P., 'Indigenous Enterprise in the Indian Coal Mining Industry, c.1835–1939', *IESHR*, 13(2), 1976, pp. 189–90.

Sivasubramonian, S., *The National Income of India in the Twentieth Century*, Oxford University Press, New Delhi, 2000.

Spodek, Howard, 'The "Manchesterisation" of Ahmedabad', *Economic Weekly*, 13 March 1965, pp. 483–84.

Srinivasan, N.R., *History of the Indian Iron and Steel Company*, published by IISCO, Burnpur, 1983.

The Economist, Millennium Issue, 23 December 1999.

Tomlinson, B.R., 'British Firms in India', mimeo, 1982.

Tripathi, Dwijendra and Jyoti Jumani, *The Concise Oxford History of Indian Business*, Oxford University Press, 2007.

Tyabji, Nasir, 'Of Traders, Usurers and British Capital: Managing Agencies and the Dalmia Jain Case', mimeo.

Tyabji, Nasir, 'Private Industry and the Second Five Year Plan: The Mundhra Episode as Exemplar of Capitalist Myopia', *Economic & Political Weekly*, 7 August 2010, pp. 47–55.

Vakil, C.N., *Economic Consequences of a Divided India: A Study of the Economies of India and Pakistan*, Vora & Co., Bombay, 1950.

INDEX